Word Weavings

Writing Poetry with Young Children

Shelley Tucker, Ph. D.

Illustrated by Joan Cottle

Good Year Books

An Imprint of Addison-Wesley Educational Publishers, Inc.

Good Year Books are available for most basic curriculum subjects plus many enrichment areas. For more Good Year Books, contact your local bookseller or educational dealer. For a complete catalog with information about other Good Year Books, please write:

Good Year Books
1900 East Lake Avenue
Glenview, IL 60025

Design by Nancy Rudd.
Front Cover: "Dance Like the Tree," by Katelyn Melvey.
Back Cover: "Jungle" by Katelyn Melvey.
Copyright © 1997 Shelley Tucker.
All Rights Reserved.
Printed in the United States of America.

ISBN 0-673-36367-8

1 2 3 4 5 6 7 8 9 - MH - 04 03 02 01 00 99 98 97

Acknowledgments

My deepest appreciation goes to the following
people: Laurie Riepe for suggesting I write poetry with
young children; Jan Wilson, Norine Gann, Pam Lewis,
Ladell Black, Elaine Jaques, Andrea Smith, and
C. C. Leonard for their delight and support;
Jamie Shilling for our creative conversations leading to
collaborations between poetry, art, song, and dance;
Margot Richardson for the bus shelter art and poetry
projects; Kathleen Coyle for designing the art in the
exercise "The Wind Is Like an Eagle"; Pam Eshelman,
Barbara Young, and Sherri Chen for all-around support
of poetry and art with children.

Thank you so much to Claudia Mauro for knowing it
is all a poem; Jackson Riepe for showing me that if
you are old enough to speak, you can compose
poetry; Laurie and Caitlin Wilson for the poetry of our
friendships; Roni Natov for reinforcing the value of
this work; Jerri Geer for her good humor and support;
Julian Riepe for his commitment to poetry and art with
young children; Terry Garrison for
living in the flow of ideas; the men and women in my
"Write from the Source Poetry Writing Workshops" for
their support of this work; my mother, Chickie
Kitchman, for encouraging the artist in me when
I was a child; and Bruce Sherman, my husband,
for sharing with me the life of the poem:
open, honest, loving, and welcoming.

In appreciation of William Stafford
who showed that poetry writing is accessible to everyone.

Contents

From *Word Weavings: Writing Poetry with Young Children* published by Good Year Books. Copyright © 1997 Shelley Tucker.

Introduction

Children are natural poets who delight in words. The language of poetry weaves easily in and out of their speech, and children can readily draw on it to compose their poems.

This book teaches poetry composition in free verse. Free verse is a type of poetry that does not use regular meter or end rhymes. It was introduced in the English language in 1855 with the publication of Walt Whitman's *Leaves of Grass*. Similar to spoken language, free verse is now the most widely used form for writing poetry. It is so natural and familiar that all children can succeed when they compose it.

Free verse provides an alternative to poetry based on standard meter, end rhymes, or set patterns. These forms are not usually integrated into children's daily language patterns, but instead are external to the ways they think and speak. What children want to say does not often fit standard poetic forms, and such poetry writing can seem difficult or meaningless to them.

When we teach poetry composition in free verse rather than with end rhymes or set meters, all children, regardless of academic ability, can readily draw on the daily rhythms of speech for use in their poems. At the same time, they discover a method of writing poetry that they can use throughout their lives.

Word Weavings teaches seven poetic elements—simile, imagery, inquiry, metaphor, personification, alliteration, and onomatopoeia—for use in free verse poetry. These are relevant and easy for children because they are already present in their everyday thoughts and language. Children derive many benefits when they use these elements to compose poetry in free verse:

1. Writing can become as easy and important as talking.

2. Children discover connections between thinking, speaking, writing, and reading.

3. Interest in reading often increases. Children want to read their poems to themselves and others.

4. These poems are generally interesting, so adults listen to them again and again. Children experience a deep sense of the importance of their words while at the same time reinforcing their reading skills.

5. Children learn to listen attentively to poetry, which improves their listening and thinking skills.

6. Writing poems makes the classroom a creative center. Words become paints without the mess. Children draw pictures with language and turn the classroom into a word gallery. Poetry writing using these poetic elements continually creates interest and enthusiasm in the classroom.

7. Poetry gives children more ways to use words in writing. Because poems draw on both figurative and literal language, children are able to express feelings, ask and answer questions, create images, and include sounds in ways often unavailable to them in other types of composition.

8. Writing poetry is active, so it makes an excellent antidote to watching television and doing other passive activities.

9. Children feel smart when they write poems with these poetic elements. Figurative language does not require the use of large words. Instead, what matters is the way the children combine everyday words to create interesting comparisons and images.

10. As children prepare their poems for publication, they see the importance of standard spelling in final drafts.

11. When children publish their poetry, their appreciation of reading and books, in general, increases.

12. Through poetry writing, children make unusual connections and create unique images that elicit praise from listeners. Children love this spontaneous surprise, delight, and affirmation. At the same time, they're not dependent on it because they often respond similarly to their own poems.

13. Creating art, making books, and reading poems extend naturally from poetry composition. These activities can be included in other subject areas too, such as science and social studies.

14. Children who compose poetry become more confident in their use of language. They take pride in their word selections, juxtapositions of sounds and rhythms, and development of ideas and images.

15. When children write poetry, they pay careful attention to their thoughts, feelings, and environment.

All children, regardless of academic accomplishment, can succeed when they compose free verse poetry based on these seven poetic elements.

From *Word Weavings: Writing Poetry with Young Children* published by Good Year Books. Copyright © 1997 Shelley Tucker.

How to Use This Book

This book is divided into seven chapters covering simile, imagery, inquiry, metaphor, personification, alliteration, and onomatopoeia. The early chapters, in general, present the simplest concepts. Each chapter begins with an introduction followed by several exercises that focus on the poetic element under discussion. Within each chapter, the exercises are arranged by level of difficulty, beginning with the easiest. One exercise, however, is not a prerequisite for another, so feel free to use them in any order. The exercises suggest ways of presenting the material, offer poetry writing activities and art projects, and close with examples of children's poetry. Children from typical school populations composed the poems that appear at the end of each exercise, and their ages are noted beside their names.

A Note About Poetic Elements

You do not need to use the terms *simile, imagery, inquiry, metaphor, personification, alliteration,* and *onomatopoeia* with young children. Instead, place the emphasis on their understanding and use of the poetic concepts. Talk with young children about the process of composition in some of the following ways:

Simile: Notice how we can say anything is like something else just by using the words *like* or *as.*

Imagery with action verbs: When we use interesting action words, we create pictures in poems.

Imagery with detailed description: One way to write a poem is to describe something carefully.

Inquiry: We can answer interesting questions in poetry.

Metaphor: A way to write poetry is to compare two things that seem different.

Personification: We compose poetry by saying that things, colors, feelings, and animals are like people. To do this, we can give objects human actions, body parts, emotions, and names, such as *she* and *he.*

Alliteration: Sometimes we write poems with words that start with the same sounds.

Onomatopoeia: We can use the sounds of people and things in our poems to make them more interesting.

Group Presentation

During the group presentation, adults ask children a variety of questions. This helps the children expand their understanding and application of the poetic concepts and shows them how to lengthen their sentences and enlarge their ideas. One measure of writing maturity is sentence length. As writing matures, sentences become longer. Consider the sentence, "I saw flowers." To lengthen it, older children and adults naturally add "Who? What? Where? When? Why?" or "How?" They might write "I saw flowers growing toward the sun or I saw flowers in a garden at the park." You can teach younger children how to extend their sentences by asking them questions about their ideas.

Another measure of academic skill is the ability to generate a variety of responses. When you ask children specific questions about their poetry, you also teach them general thinking skills. As they internalize this process, the children learn to ask the questions themselves.

Dance like...

Writing Poetry
Children Recording Their Poems

After the group presentation, many young children can write their poems by themselves. To support their flow of ideas, have them initially use inventive, made-up, or guess-and-go spellings when they are unsure of standard spellings. This supports their creativity and production in first drafts. Work with them later on standard spellings for final drafts.

Adults Taking Dictation

Young children frequently need other people to record their poems. When young children watch adults and older children take dictation, they observe that writing can be as easy as thinking and speaking. They see how to use standard sentence punctuation and capitalization. Children also learn about editing when their poems are reread to them.

Follow these steps to record children's poetry:

1. Ask the children general questions first. In the exercise "Glide Like a Bicycle," for example, begin by asking, "How do you want to start your poem?"

2. Record their responses. If the children do not know how they want to begin their poems, read them the line starts listed in the exercise.

Example:

Do you want to start your poem with "Leap like," "Soar like," "Fly like," or "Glide like"?

(Some children need fewer choices. Then offer two line starts and have them choose one.)

From *Word Weavings: Writing Poetry with Young Children* published by Good Year Books. Copyright © 1997 Shelley Tucker.

3. After children begin their lines, ask another general question, such as, "What do you want to say next?"

4. Record their answers. If they have none, choose three categories suggested in the exercise, and ask them to make their selection.

> **Example:**
>
> Do you want to name a color, an animal, or some kind of weather?
>
> (If children need fewer options, choose a familiar category, such as animals or colors, and tell them to name one.)

5. Ask a final question to show children that they can easily continue to extend their sentences just by answering questions.

> **Example:**
>
> Child   Leap like the wind.
> Adult: Where?
> Child: In the sky.

6. Record their answers.

> **Example**
>
> Leap like the wind in the sky.

7. Read aloud each sentence that they compose. At the end of the dictation, read the entire poem aloud too.

Titles

Most poems written by young children do not require titles. Their poetry is usually short, so their topics do not need a summary or an explanation. If you want children to compose titles, however, suggest that they:

- select one or more words from their poems for the title; or
- describe what their poems are about in their titles.

Evaluation

Do not use letter or number evaluations on children's poems. When graded, children often come to believe in "good" or "bad" poets and think only some people are able to write well. To support children's natural abilities to compose poetry, encourage them with feedback. Comment on:

- specific words and topics you like and why;
- how you feel when you hear or read their poems;
- what you think about as you listen to their poetry; and
- how much you appreciate their writing in general.

Making Art

Art and poetry are natural companions. Both rely on elements of color, texture, dimension, comparison, attention, and surprise. Each exercise is presented so that the children compose poetry first and then create art. This way, they gather ideas for their art as they write. To follow this sequence, show children samples of the art during group presentations, and give them specific instructions for making the art after they write. The children, however, could also do art before writing.

All of the art projects in this book require inexpensive or free supplies. Most of the materials are readily available in classrooms and supply rooms. You can easily collect the others. Parents make excellent resources, and some local stores give free supplies, such as grocery bags and old keys, to educators. Some useful arts and crafts materials are grouped by category in the box at the right.

This key opens the sky.

Containers

- milk containers
- egg cartons
- margarine tubs
- plastic milk, juice, and water bottles in all sizes
- shoe boxes
- aluminum foil
- paper bags in a variety of sizes

Craft Store Supplies

- craft sticks
- confetti
- colored tissue paper

Food

- uncooked pasta
- beans

Hardware

- keys
- miscellaneous hardware, such as doorknobs

Paper

- canceled stamps
- paper plates
- magazines
- calendars
- greeting cards
- brochures
- wrapping paper
- Contact® paper
- tagboard
- writing paper
- construction paper
- cardboard
- old maps
- catalogs

Sewing Materials

- buttons
- zippers

Things Found Outside

- shells
- sand
- rocks
- stones
- leaves
- branches
- twigs
- pine cones

From *Word Weavings: Writing Poetry with Young Children* published by Good Year Books. Copyright © 1997 Shelley Tucker.

Collecting and Showing Poetry and Art

Making Books

Children know that everything with a binding is a book. You can easily make books with them, and the benefits extend throughout the language arts curriculum. Making books clearly shows children the value of thinking, speaking, writing, publishing, and reading. It integrates process with product, letting children see the relationship between the abstract and the concrete. Children feel proud when they make books and look for opportunities to read them to others.

Here are four ways to make books with children to include their poetry and artwork. Between book covers:

1. Staple sheets of paper together on the left sides or at the tops.

2. Stack sheets of paper, fold them in half, and staple them in the center.

3. Take a stack of paper, fold in it half, and punch holes on the left side through the folds. Use yarn, ribbon, or string to make the bindings.

4. Use comb binding machines available in most schools.

There are also wonderful, decorative books that can include the poetry of one or many children. Please see the reference section at the back of this book for suggestions on bookmaking resources.

Reading Aloud

Reading aloud is another important part of the poetry process. It shows children that their words matter. It strengthens their reading skills while at the same time increasing their comfort with oral presentations. Reading aloud allows children to hear ways to edit their poems. It also transforms the classroom into a community where children pay close attention to each other's words, interests, feelings, and ideas. Give many opportunities for children to read their poetry aloud to classmates and adults.

Young children can read or present their poems in several ways. They can:

- read their poetry without assistance,

- have another person read their poems aloud,

- have someone say their words aloud to them and then repeat them, and

- read what they can and have someone else read the rest of their poetry with them.

Displaying Art and Poems

Children are thrilled when their art is shown. Here are some ways to display their poetry and art:

- Attach poems to the back of art.

- Suspend poems from the bottom of art.

- Mount poetry and related art in adjacent spaces on bulletin boards.

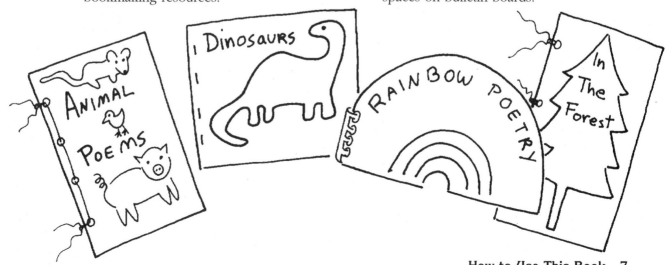

Simile

A *simile* compares two unlike nouns using *like* or *as*.

Similes are a staple of our everyday talk. Like the air we breathe, they are so common we hardly notice them. Consider, for example, the following similes:

The sun feels as warm as a blanket.
A home run ball looks like the moon.
A book is like a friend.

Children remember and appreciate similes in their poems because they are made of nouns. Most nouns create visual images, so even a single one in a poem is easy to recall. The images suggested by the two nouns in a simile create an entire photograph. Brianna drew interesting comparisons between the nouns in her poem and created a small photo album of word pictures. Now, at age seven, Brianna readily remembers her poem.

"Curved as a Turtle's Shell," the first model in this chapter, is a presimile exercise. By adding only one noun, children can get a feel for writing similes. In the other exercises, they compose similes using both nouns.

Easy and fun to write, similes flower in children's poems like daffodils of creativity.

MICE

Mice are like the night

playing hide and go seek

in the shadows.

Mice are like the day

sleeping under the warm sun.

Briana du Nann, age 5

From *Word Weavings: Writing Poetry with Young Children* published by Good Year Books. Copyright © 1997 Shelley Tucker.

Curved as a Turtle's Shell

Description

Children notice the shapes of things. They know that the roundness of the moon, the arc of a rainbow, and the curve of a stone are important characteristics of these objects.

In this exercise, children compose poetry about things that are round or curved. They then illustrate their poems with three-dimensional art.

Presentation

Write the following words on the board and review them with the children:

> round as   curved as

Ask them to start with the phrase "round as" and add the name of a fruit or vegetable.

> *Examples:*   round as an orange
> round as a grape

Next have them begin with the phrase "round as" and add the name of something round on a bicycle, car, or bus.

> *Examples:*   round as a wheel
> round as a bus tire

After a few responses, ask the following questions to show the children ways to extend their ideas:

> *Where? When? Doing what? Looks like what?*

> *Example:*   **CHILD:** *Round as a wheel.*
> **TEACHER:** *Doing what?*
> **SAME OR ANOTHER CHILD:** *Moving faster and faster.*
> **TEACHER:** *We can put both parts together and say, "Round as a wheel moving faster and faster."*

Art Materials

- Construction paper

- Pencils, crayons, or markers

- Glue

- Round objects such as confetti, small hardware, buttons, small wheels, lentils, bottle caps, pictures from magazines

- Curved shapes, such as ribbon, string, yarn, beans, pasta

Practice

Now repeat the process using the phrase "curved as."

- Choose one of the following categories:

animals	*things in the sky*
things outside the window	*weather*
musical instruments	*bodies of water*

- Have the children start with the phrase "curved as" and add an example from that category.

- Then ask the following questions to help them extend their ideas:

Where? When? Doing what? Looks like what?

(With practice, the children will learn to combine the phrases by themselves.)

- Repeat the steps using other categories.

Writing Poetry

Tell the children to write or say poems, starting with the phrases "round as" and "curved as." Review the categories used in the presentation to remind them of some things they might name.

Making Art

Give the children round and curved objects. Have them glue bottle caps and lids, pieces of construction paper, magazine pictures, confetti, beans, nuts and bolts, ribbons, yarn, or pasta on paper to create, for example, the slope of a mountain, the curve of a bike wheel, or the arc of a camel's back.

**Based on art by
Amelia Gallagher,
age 7**

From *Word Weavings: Writing Poetry with Young Children* published by Good Year Books. Copyright © 1997 Shelley Tucker.

Round as a turtle shell,

hard and protected.

Curved as a snake

slithering in the desert.

Sam Winninghoff, age 7

RIBBON

A ribbon is as curved

as a bending-over leaf,

as round as the moon

shining down on the water,

as curved as a snake

curling up for a winter nap.

Michelle Nevins, age 6

THE WORLD

Round as the world

wearing glasses

at the beach.

Harry Howell, age 5

Curved as a worm in the ground.

Round as the sun in the sky.

Curved as mountains

with snow on them.

Round as a seed underground

waiting to grow.

Meaghan McClure, age 5

CURVED AS MOONLIGHT

Curved as the wind

as it fights against the rain.

Round as music

as the notes float past.

Curved as moonlight in the sky.

Mollie Price, age 8

Leaves Look Like Stars

Art Materials

- Construction paper

- Pencils, crayons, or markers

- Glue

- Fresh or dried leaves, stencils of leaves, metallic confetti in the shape of leaves, or pictures of leaves

Description

Look at leaves, and it's easy to see the shapes of feathers, arrows, and stars. The colors, textures, sizes, contours, and smells of leaves suggest ideas for children's poetry.

In this activity, you or the children collect different kinds of leaves. The children then write or dictate poems comparing the leaves to a variety of things. Next, they use actual leaves or leaf shapes in their art.

Presentation

Write the following phrases on the board and review them with the children:

leaves look like	*leaves seem like*	*leaves sound like*
leaves feel like	*leaves smell like*	*leaves move like*

Then hold up a leaf. Tell the children that leaves sometimes look like other things. Ask them to start with the phrase "leaves look like" and then complete the sentence naming something in the sky.

Examples:

> *Leaves look like birds.*
> *Leaves look like planets.*

After a few responses, ask some of the following questions to show the children how to extend their ideas:

> *Where? When? Why? How? Doing what?*

Examples:

> **CHILD:** *Leaves look like birds.*
> **TEACHER:** *Doing what?*
> **SAME OR ANOTHER CHILD:** *Flying in the air.*
> **TEACHER:** *We can put both parts together and say, "Leaves look birds flying in the air."*

Now choose another leaf and show it to the children. Suggest that they compare leaves to things in the ocean. Have the children start with the phrase "leaves feel like" and complete the sentence naming something in the ocean.

From *Word Weavings: Writing Poetry with Young Children* published by Good Year Books. Copyright © 1997 Shelley Tucker.

> *Leaves feel like coral.*
> *Leaves feel like waves.*

After a few responses, ask the children some of the following questions to show them how to extend their ideas:

> *Where? When? Why? How? Doing what?*

Example:

> **CHILD:** *Leaves feel like coral.*
> **TEACHER:** *When do leaves feel like coral?*
> **SAME OR ANOTHER CHILD:** *When they're wet.*
> **TEACHER:** *Who can put both parts together?*
> **CHILD OR TEACHER:** *Leaves feel like coral when they're wet.*

(With practice, the children will learn to combine the phrases by themselves.)

Practice

Provide the children with more practice by doing this exercise:

■ List the following categories on the board and choose one:

> *weather*   *holidays*
> *fruits and vegetables* *animals*
> *machines*

■ Have the children start with the phrase "leaves sound like" and add an example from that category.

■ Ask some questions to show them how to extend their sentences.

■ Repeat the steps using the phrases "leaves seem like," "leaves smell like," and "leaves move like," instead of "leaves sound like."

Writing Poetry

Tell the children to write or say poems that start with the phrases on the board. They may choose which ones to use. Remind them that they might compare leaves to things in the sky, weather, objects in bodies of water, fruits and vegetable, animals, holidays, machines, and anything else that suggests leaves.

Making Art

Have the children use actual leaves, pictures of leaves, or shapes of leaves to make collages or do crayon rubbings. They might also use leaves to illustrate the comparisons in their poems. For example, if a child writes "leaves feel like porcupine quills," she might draw a porcupine with quills made of leaves.

Leaves feel like the grass in Hawaii.

Leaves look like little oak trees

in the forest.

Leaves smell good like honey.

Briana Brewer, age 6

LEAVES

Leaves feel like the wind blowing

in the summer over my red house.

Leaves move like raindrops

falling from the sky onto a bird flying north.

Leaves sound like snowflakes falling in winter.

Leaves feel like rain coming from the sky

splashing in puddles in the spring.

Rachel Milligan, age 5

PORCUPINE LEAVES

Leaves feel like a porcupine

walking slowly on the ground.

Leaves move like a bumpy dinosaur.

Leaves sound wonderful

when they fall in love.

Meaghan McClure, age 5

Leaves smell like maple syrup on my pancakes

on a cold winter Saturday.

Leaves sound like a fox running fast in the grass

on a breezy summer day.

Leaves look like shells when they are broken

and laying on the beach after a windstorm.

Leah Perlmutter, age 5

From *Word Weavings: Writing Poetry with Young Children* published by Good Year Books. Copyright © 1997 Shelley Tucker.

Ribbons Sound Like Rain

Description

Ribbons and bows provide a parade of textures, colors, and sounds.

In this exercise, the children compare ribbons and bows to other things, such as the outline of a cat or the crunch of snow. Then they use the ribbons and bows in their art to illustrate their poems.

Presentation

Write the following words on the board and review them with the children:

> a ribbon   a bow

Then pick up a pile of ribbons and move it back and forth. Tell the children that ribbons sometimes look like animals. Have them start with the words "a ribbon looks like" and name an animal.

Examples:
> A ribbon looks like a snake.
> A ribbon looks like a bird.

After a few responses, ask some of the following questions to show the children how to lengthen their sentences:

> Where? When? Why? How? Doing what?

Example:
> **CHILD:** *A ribbon looks like a snake.*
> **TEACHER:** *Doing what?*
> **SAME OR ANOTHER CHILD:** *Slithering in the grass.*
> **TEACHER:** *We can put both parts together and say, "A ribbon looks like a snake slithering in the grass."*

Art Materials

- Construction paper
- Pencils, crayons, or markers
- Glue
- Ribbons and bows (Yarn, string, or streamers may be used instead of ribbons and bows.)

Ask the children to start with the words "a ribbon moves like" and add the name of some kind of weather.

Examples:

> *A ribbon moves like a tornado.*
> *A white ribbon moves like the snow falling.*

After a few responses, ask some of the following questions to show them how to extend their lines:

> *Where? When? Why? How? How are they moving?*

Example:

> **CHILD:** *A ribbon moves like a tornado.*
> **TEACHER:** *How?*
> **SAME OR ANOTHER CHILD:** *Twisting.*
> **TEACHER:** *Who can put both parts together?*
> **CHILD OR TEACHER:** *A ribbon moves like a tornado twisting.*

(With practice, the children will learn to combine the phrases by themselves.)

Practice

Then provide the children with more practice comparing ribbons to other things.

■ List the following categories on the board and choose one:

> *foods   holidays*
> *things in the sky   emotions*
> *transportation   things in the ocean*
> *things that grow outside*

■ Have the children start with the phrase "a ribbon feels like," and add an example from the category.

■ Then ask some of the following questions to show them how to extend their ideas:

> *Where? When? Why? How? Doing what?*

■ Repeat the steps using phrases about bows:

> *a bow sounds like   a bow bends like   a bow seems like*

From *Word Weavings: Writing Poetry with Young Children* published by Good Year Books. Copyright © 1997 Shelley Tucker.

Writing Poetry

Tell the children to write or say poems about ribbons and bows. Write the following words on the board to encourage them to use different verbs in their poems:

> *sounds like*
> *looks like*
> *feels like*
> *moves like*
> *seems like*
> *bends like*

Making Art

Ask the children to create art using ribbons and bows. For example, if a child writes "a ribbon moves like a waterfall," he could use a ribbon in the picture to show water flowing down a mountain. Another child who says, "a bow looks like a star," might place a bow high in the sky. The ribbons and bows can also be used in abstract pictures, like paints adding texture and color to art.

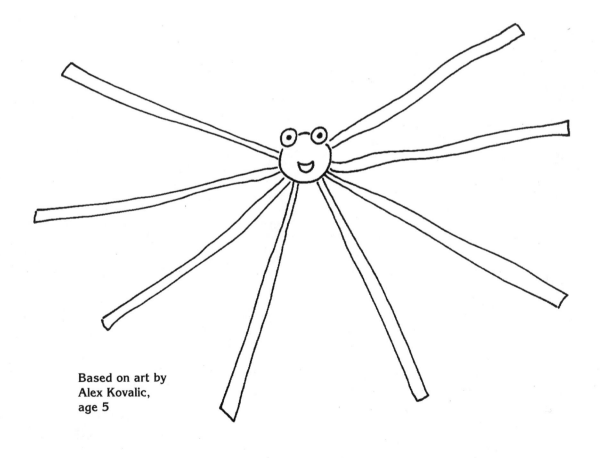

**Based on art by
Alex Kovalic,
age 5**

PUDDLE OF COLOR

Ribbons are like a puddle of color.

A poem is like a ribbon

traveling along your fingers.

Johannas Heller, age 6

A bow is like a flower
and a ribbon is like a horse's tail.
Ribbons move like a stream
flowing down a mountain.

Casey Ikeda, age 5

FIREWORKS

A ribbon pops in the sky
and does fireworks.
A ribbon looks like purple,
pink, and green exercising.

Kyle Blake, age 5

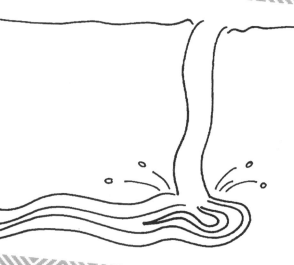

A bow sounds like the rain
pitter pattering on the roof.
A ribbon moves like a snake.
A bow looks like a snowflake
falling from the sky.

Angela Potter, age 5

BOWS AND RIBBONS

Bows are like crackling fire.
Ribbons sound

like rumbling snow.

Osani Shapiro, age 5

From *Word Weavings: Writing Poetry with Young Children* published by Good Year Books. Copyright © 1997 Shelley Tucker.

Red Smells Like Strawberries

Description

We do not only see colors. We also sense their smells, tastes, textures, and sounds.

In this exercise, children write about the feel, sound, smell, and appearance of colors. Then they make collages to illustrate their poems.

Presentation

Ask the children to name colors.

Write the following verb phrases on the board:

feels like	*looks like*	*sounds like*
tastes like	*smells like*	

Have the children select a color and describe what it feels like.

Examples:
> *Yellow feels like the sun.*
> *Green feels like grass.*
> *Red feels like love.*

After a few responses, ask some of the following questions to show them ways to extend their ideas:

> *Where? When? Why? Doing what?*

Example:
> **CHILD:** *Yellow feels like the sun.*
> **TEACHER:** *When?*
> **SAME OR ANOTHER CHILD:** *In the morning.*
> **TEACHER:** *We can put both parts together and say, "Yellow feels like the sun in the morning."*

(With practice, children will learn to combine phrases by themselves.)

From *Word Weavings: Writing Poetry with Young Children* published by Good Year Books. Copyright © 1997 Shelley Tucker.

Art Materials

- Construction paper
- Pencils, crayons, or markers
- Scissors
- Glue
- Assorted paper for collages: greeting cards, calendars, pictures from old magazines, Contact® paper, wallpaper, decorative paper bags, comics, wrapping paper

Practice

Repeat these steps to give children more practice:

- Choose a verb phrase from the list.

- Have the children say a color, add the verb phrase, and then complete the sentence.

- Ask the following questions to show them how to extend their ideas:

> *Where? When? Why? Doing what?*

Writing Poetry

Tell the children to write or say poems about how colors taste, feel, sound, smell, and look. Have them use the verb phrases on the board in their poems.

Making Art

The world is full of beautifully colored paper and pictures waiting to be recycled in collages. Give the children old wrapping paper, wallpaper, decorative bags, pictures from magazines, aluminum foil, greeting cards, calendars, and colorful comics. Have them cut out shapes from this assortment of paper and glue them onto construction paper to make collages that highlight their poems.

From *Word Weavings: Writing Poetry with Young Children* published by Good Year Books. Copyright © 1997 Shelley Tucker.

Red tastes like raspberries

on a cake.

Blue smells like the ocean

and the sky.

Green feels like grass

at my baseball game.

Yellow looks like gold

in the sunset.

Levona Johnson, age 6

White sounds like the wind

blowing through the grass.

Tosten Haugerud, age 7

Red looks like a strawberry.

Blue tastes like a river.

Purple feels like salt water.

Green sounds like leaves

falling off trees.

Gabriel Sasnet, age 7

COLORS

Red smells like a flower

in the spring.

Black feels like a cat

in the fog.

Blue looks like a bluebird

flying in the sky.

Turquoise seems like water

in the afternoon.

Yellow looks like the sun

on a bright summer morning.

All the colors mixed together

on a rainy, sunny day

make a rainbow.

Ryann McChesney, age 5

Orange sounds like it's growing

on the ground.

Blue feels like a blue jay flying.

Brown looks like a bear

catching a fish.

Red feels like fireworks

blooming in the sky.

Hanah Lee Ho, age 5

From *Word Weavings: Writing Poetry with Young Children* published by Good Year Books. Copyright © 1997 Shelley Tucker.

The Wind Is Like an Eagle

Art Materials

- Construction paper, 12 by 18 inches (approximately 30 by 45 cm), 2 sheets per child

- Pencils, crayons, or markers

- Scissors

- Stapler

- Dowels, plastic sticks, or branches

- Strips of paper, 1 by 24 inches to 36 inches (approximately 2.54 cm by 60 to 90 cm) each

Description

Children often see similarities between our natural surroundings and animals. Hail hops like a rabbit, a river is shaped like a snake, or a tree feels as solid as an elephant.

In this exercise, the children compare stars, stones, and other natural phenomena with animals. Then they assemble three-dimensional paper animals to illustrate their poems.

Presentation

Choose some of the following categories and list them horizontally across the board:

> *things that grow in forests*
> *weather*
> *things in the sky*
> *objects in the ocean and on the beach*
> *seasons*
> *bodies of water*

Ask the children to give examples and write their suggestions under the categories. Then have them name animals. List these on the board too.

Now ask the children to select a nature word and add the name of an animal that is like it in some way. They may use the words on the board or suggest new ones.

Examples:
> *A cloud is like a cat.*
> *The wind is like a bird.*
> *A mountain is like a rhinoceros.*

Sometimes the children will name the animal first, and that's fine.

After a few responses, ask some of the following questions to show the children how to extend their ideas:

> *Where? When? Why? How? Doing what? How are they alike?*

Example:

> **CHILD:** *A cloud is like a cat.*
> **TEACHER:** *How are they alike?*
> **SAME OR ANOTHER CHILD:** *They're soft and fluffy.*
> **TEACHER:** *We can put both parts together and say,*
> *"A cloud is like a cat. They're soft and fluffy."*

Example including all of the steps:

> **TEACHER:** *Who will name something in nature other than an animal?*
> **CHILD:** *Trees.*
> **TEACHER:** *Who will start with the words, "Trees are like," and add the name of an animal that in some way reminds you of trees?*
> **SAME OR ANOTHER CHILD:** *Trees are like birds.*
> **TEACHER:** *Where?*
> **SAME OR ANOTHER CHILD:** *In the wind.*
> **TEACHER:** *Who can put both parts together?*
> **CHILD OR TEACHER:** *Trees are like birds in the wind.*

(After some practice, the children will learn to combine phrases by themselves.)

Practice

Repeat the process to give the children more practice.

- Ask them to name something in nature.

- Have the children add an animal that is in some way like it.

- Ask a few of the following questions to show them how to extend their ideas:

> *Where? When? Why? How? Doing what? How are they alike?*

Writing Poetry

Tell the children to describe something in nature by comparing it to an animal. Then have them extend their ideas. They may use the words on the board or select different ones for their poems.

Making Art

Give each child two pieces of construction paper, 12 by 18 inches (30 by 45 cm) each. Ask the children to draw an animal from their poems on one piece and decorate it. Then have them cut out their animals in duplicate.

Show the children how to tape a stick on the back of one animal cut-out so that part of the stick extends beyond the shape. Then have them staple the two identical animals together with the stick inside.

Next, the children can make folded legs for their animals. Starting with two strips of paper per leg measuring 1 by 24 to 36 inches (2.54 cm by 60 to 90 cm) each, you or another adult staple the ends of the strips together so they're perpendicular. Have the children fold the bottom strip over the top one and crease it, repeating the process until both strips are completely folded, one over the other. After making as many legs as needed, have the children tape one end of each leg to their animals. The children now have stick puppets to accompany their poems.

Based on art by Ben Lukes, age 7

From *Word Weavings: Writing Poetry with Young Children* published by Good Year Books. Copyright © 1997 Shelley Tucker.

CHEETAH

A cheetah running
is like electricity.

Johannas Heller, age 6

CLOUD

One night I went out for a walk
when I saw a cloud shaped like a horse.
It jumped six feet off the ground
and kicked its hooves.
Then it wagged its tail
and seemed to be eating hay.

Maggie Hatcher, age 9

Ice is like frogs
slippery and wet.
Turtles are lumpy
just like the moon.

Kevin McKenna, age 8

FALL

Fall is like a snake
shedding his skin.

Aaron Graham, age 7

Water is like a bunny
hopping and jumping
over the rocks.

The moon is like a bobcat
slipping across the sky.

Anna Crandall, age 7

From *Word Weavings: Writing Poetry with Young Children* published by Good Year Books. Copyright © 1997 Shelley Tucker.

Summer Tastes Like Ice Cream

From *Word Weavings: Writing Poetry with Young Children* published by Good Year Books. Copyright © 1997 Shelley Tucker.

Art Materials

- Construction paper, one piece per child

- Pencils, crayons, or markers

- Scissors

- Glue and tape

- Strips of construction paper one inch wide in a contrasting color for weaving

- Scraps of construction paper in assorted colors for drawing pictures

Description

Children remember the sights, tastes, smells, and sounds of the seasons. A hot summer day might be rich and thick like ice cream. Winter might remind them of a blanket of snow. Spring could seem like a white tulip curved as the moon and autumn like rain made of leaves.

In this exercise, children describe the seasons. They then make comparisons between their descriptions and other things. Next, they weave paper mats in seasonal colors and glue illustrations of their poems to them.

Presentation

Have the children name the seasons and write them in a horizontal row across the board. Then ask them to name things, such as weather, sports, holidays, colors, and animal behaviors, that remind them of each season. List their suggestions under the season names.

Choose one topic from the board and ask the children to suggest a first line for a poem about it.

Example:

> **TEACHER:** *Who will start a poem about snow?*
> **CHILD:** *I love snow in January.*

Select a noun from the child's sentence. Choose one the children can easily visualize. In this example, the word *snow* suggests strong images. Name a feature of snow, such as its color, temperature, or shape. Then have the children suggest other objects with the same characteristic.

Example:

> **TEACHER:** *Who will name something else that is white like snow?*
> **FIRST CHILD:** *A cloud.*
> **SECOND CHILD:** *A blanket.*
> **THIRD CHILD:** *Whipped cream.*

Show the children how they can use these comparisons in a poem:

> **TEACHER:** *We might say, "I love snow in January because it's like whipped cream." We could also say, "I love snow in January. It covers the ground like a blanket."*

Now have the children add a second line to the poem.

Example:

> **TEACHER:** *Who will add another sentence to the poem about snow?*
> **CHILD:** *I ride a sled in the snow on Saturday.*

Select a vivid noun from the child's sentence. In the example above, the word *sled* creates a clear picture. Choose a characteristic of the sled, and have the children name other objects with that trait.

> **TEACHER:** *What moves like a sled?*
> **FIRST CHILD:** *A magic carpet.*
> **SECOND CHILD:** *A jet.*
> **THIRD CHILD:** *Ice skates.*

Demonstrate how to make the comparisons in the poem.

Example:

> **TEACHER:** *We might say, "I ride a sled in the snow on Saturday, and it moves like a magic carpet." We could also write, "I ride a sled in the snow on Saturday, flying like a jet."*

Then review the final poem.

> **TEACHER:** *Here's a poem using some of our ideas. Notice that we describe the snow and a sled by saying they're like other things:*
>
> > *I love snow in January*
> > *because it's like whipped cream.*
> > *I ride a sled in the snow on Saturday,*
> > *flying like a jet.*

From *Word Weavings: Writing Poetry with Young Children* published by Good Year Books. Copyright © 1997 Shelley Tucker.

Practice

Repeat this process many times to give the children more practice writing seasonal poems that include comparisons.

- Choose a topic from the board.

- Ask the children to compose a first sentence for a poem about that subject.

- Select a noun they can easily picture.

- Name a trait of that noun such as its shape, function, size, or color. Ask the children to name objects with that trait.

- Review the sentence making comparisons between the original noun and the other things the children named.

- Have them form their own sentences including comparisons.

- Ask the children to suggest a second sentence for the poem.

- Repeat the steps to create more comparisons.

- Review the whole poem.

Writing Poetry

Tell the children to write or say poems about the seasons. Have them choose topics and decide how they will start their poems. Remind the children to select a thing from each sentence and then describe how it is like something else.

Making Art

Have the children fold their sheets of construction paper in half. To prepare papers for weaving, they make cuts every 1 to 2 inches, starting at the fold and stopping 1 inch from the opposite end. Then they weave the strips of paper through the sheets. These woven mats become the backgrounds for their art.

Ask the children to make pictures to illustrate their poems. They then cut out these drawings and glue them onto the weavings. The woven mats show the colors of the seasons, and the contrasts between dimensions, textures, and subjects within their pictures emphasize the comparisons in their poems.

From *Word Weavings: Writing Poetry with Young Children* published by Good Year Books. Copyright © 1997 Shelley Tucker.

In the spring, the sky

looks like a flowing river.

In the fall, the leaves

look like the wind

blowing like a rainbow.

Melissa Chen, age 7

In winter, the snow looks like doughnut powder.

In winter, the snow looks like big chunks

of vanilla ice cream.

Sometimes in summer, the brown crayons melt

and look like creamy chocolate.

Harry Howell, age 5

IN FALL

You make big piles of leaves

to jump in,

like jumping in the stars.

Sophie Baird-Daniel, age 6

Fall is like the wind

rushing through the trees

on a cold, cold night.

Winter is like a bear

creeping through the fog.

Lucas Powers, age 8

SEASONS

Winter's snowflakes sound like

musical instruments when they are falling.

Spring is like an arrow coming and going.

Summer is like a single sun

shining on the earth.

Montana Tippett, age 8

From *Word Weavings: Writing Poetry with Young Children* published by Good Year Books. Copyright © 1997 Shelley Tucker.

Imagery

Imagery is the creation of pictures with words.

LEAP

Leap like a pencil

as it writes each letter.

Soar like a name

as it goes on a piece of paper.

Glide like a leaf

as it falls off a tree.

Leap like the waves

as they crash along the beach.

Fly like happy

as it goes through your mind.

Katelyn Melvey, age 7

Imagery is the process of turning words into pictures. Writing similes is one way to create images. You can also paint pictures with words by writing detailed descriptions and using interesting action verbs.

Two of the exercises in this chapter give children experience describing things in detail. In "Dinosaur House," they create imaginary homes. "Hills Are Shaped Like Bananas" uses children's observation skills and shows them how to include comparisons in their descriptions.

All of the other exercises encourage the children to start their sentences with vivid action verbs. Read the helping verb _is_ and no picture comes to mind. Look at the action verb _soar_ on the other hand, and it evokes the image of an eagle gliding through the air or a basketball moving toward the hoop. By starting with interesting action verbs such as _glide, fly, paint,_ and _weave,_ children create pictures in their poems with words.

From _Word Weavings: Writing Poetry with Young Children_ published by Good Year Books. Copyright © 1997 Shelley Tucker.

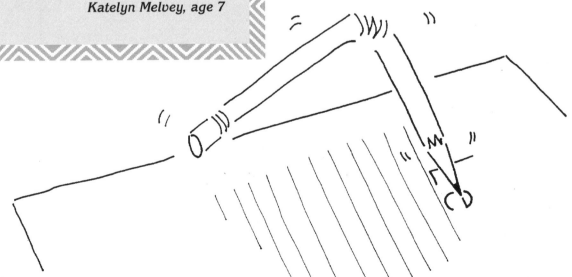

Glide Like a Bicycle

Description

Just say the word *leap* and notice how it jumps out of your mouth. The word *fly* takes flight, *glide* rolls along, and *soar* spreads wings.

In this exercise, children use the natural rhythms of the words *leap, fly, glide,* and *soar* to describe the movements of things. Then they draw pictures, cut them out in duplicate, stuff them, and suspend them on mobiles.

Presentation

Write the following words on the board and review them with the children:

> *leap like*
> *fly like*
> *glide like*
> *soar like*

Have them start with the phrase "leap like" and add the name of some kind of weather.

Examples:
> Leap like the wind.
> Leap like the rain.

After a few responses, ask some of the following questions to show them how to extend their ideas:

> *Where? When? Why? How? Doing what?*

Example:
> **CHILD:** *Leap like the wind.*
> **TEACHER:** *Where?*
> **SAME OR ANOTHER CHILD:** *In a storm.*
> **TEACHER:** *We can put the two parts together, and say, "Leap like the wind in a storm."*

Art Materials

- Large grocery bags
- Pencils, crayons, or markers
- Scissors
- Stapler
- Hole punch
- String
- Beans
- Dowels, plastic sticks, or branches for mobiles

Then have the children start with the words "soar like," and add the name of a color.

Examples:	Soar like blue. Soar like yellow.

After a few responses, ask some of the following questions to show the children how to lengthen their ideas:

> *Where? When? Why? How? Doing what? Going where?*
> *Going into what? Leaving what?*

Example:	CHILD: *Soar like blue.* TEACHER: *Going into what?* SAME OR ANOTHER CHILD: *The sky.* TEACHER: *Who can put the two parts together?* CHILD OR TEACHER: *Soar like blue going into the sky.*

(With practice, children will learn to combine the phrases by themselves.)

Practice

Provide the children with more practice by doing this exercise:

■ List the following categories on the board and choose one:

> *weather*
> *things in the ocean*
> *objects in the sky*
> *things that grow outside*
> *months*
> *transportation*

■ Have the children start with the words "fly like," and add an example from that category.

■ Then ask some of the following questions to show them how to extend their ideas:

> *Where? When? Why? How? Doing what?*

■ Repeat the steps using the words "glide like" instead of "fly like." Then use both line starts again with different categories.

Writing Poetry

Tell the children to write or say poems, starting lines in their poems with the phrases "leap like," "fly like," "glide like," and "soar like." They may decide which words to use and in what order. Review the categories with them. Remind the children of the questions to show them how to extend their ideas.

Making Art

In this art project, the children draw shapes, stuff them with beans, and suspend them on mobiles. Prepare the following for each child: Cut out the fronts and backs of large grocery bags, and cut these in half. Fold each half in half.

Then have the children draw the shape of something from their poems on one half of the paper and cut out these shapes in duplicate. Next, ask them to punch holes in the centers near the tops of the two shapes. Then instruct them to staple together the bottoms and sides of the duplicate shapes, leaving enough room to put in beans. After they insert the beans between the shapes, have them staple the tops shut. Next, ask them to put string through the holes. Mount the string on dowels, branches, or plastic sticks to make mobiles, moving art that leaps, soars, flies, and glides.

Soar like a leaf

falling off a tree in fall.

Fly like a cougar

jumping from a mountain.

Glide like lightning

running across the sky.

Soar like the months of the year.

Montana Tippett, age 8

Fly like a flower

going to a garden.

Glide like a bird

flying to a seed.

Leap like a horse

jumping in the wind.

Joy of the people

cheer for the year.

Briar Schwartz, Age 6

Fly like a bird across the seashore.

Leap like a frog in the mud.

Soar like an airplane in the sky.

Glide like white in the wind.

Fly like flower petals through the trees.

Alison Haruta, age 6

SOAR LIKE A BIRD

Soar like a bird catching its prey.

Fly like a butterfly in summer.

Leap like the wind

jumping the midnight sky.

Sophie Baird-Daniel, age 5

LEAP LIKE AN ANTELOPE

Leap like an antelope

in the forest thinking about home.

Fly like red in the sky at night.

Soar like the rain

pouring on the world.

Gabriel Sasnet, age 8

Dance Like Yellow

Description

Trees, oceans, and refrigerators can sing, paint, draw, and dance onto the paper through words.

In this exercise, children begin lines of their poems with the phrases "dance like," "paint like," "draw like," and "sing like." Then they make paper windsocks to illustrate the movement in their poetry.

Presentation

Write the following phrases on the board and review them with the children:

> *dance like*
> *paint like*
> *draw like*
> *sing like*

Tell them that in a poem we might say, "Dance like the girls and boys." Poetry also allows us to write more unusual things, such as "Dance like the rain" and "Dance like spaghetti." Have the children start with the words "dance like" and add the name of something in the sky.

Examples: *Dance like the sun.*
Dance like the clouds.

After a few responses, ask the children some of the following questions to show them how to extend their ideas:

> *Where? When? Why? How?*

Example:
CHILD: *Dance like the sun.*
TEACHER: *When?*
SAME OR ANOTHER CHILD: *In the summer.*
TEACHER: *We can put the two parts together and say, "Dance like the sun in the summer."*

From *Word Weavings: Writing Poetry with Young Children* published by Good Year Books. Copyright © 1997 Shelley Tucker.

Art Materials

- Butcher paper, 4 to 8 feet (approximately 1.2 m by 2.4 m) per child

- Pencils, crayons, or markers

- Scissors

- Stapler

- String, pipe cleaners

Then ask the children to start with the phrase "paint like" and add the name of an animal.

Examples:

> *Paint like a cat.*
> *Paint like a lion.*

After a few responses, ask some of the following questions to show them how to extend their ideas:

> *Where? When? Why? How?*

Example:

> **CHILD:** *Paint like a cat.*
> **TEACHER:** *Where?*
> **SAME OR ANOTHER CHILD:** *In a tree.*
> **TEACHER:** *Who can put the two parts together?*
> **CHILD OR TEACHER:** *Paint like a cat in a tree.*

(With practice, the children will learn to combine the phrases by themselves.)

Practice

Provide the children more practice by doing this exercise:

■ List the following categories on the board and choose one:

> *holidays*
> *bodies of water*
> *things you can see out a window*
> *weather*
> *months and seasons*

■ Have the children start with the phrase "paint like" and add an example from that category.

■ After a few responses, ask some of the following questions to show the children how to extend their ideas:

> *Where? When? Why? How?*

■ Repeat the steps using the phrases "draw like" and "sing like" in place of "paint like."

From *Word Weavings: Writing Poetry with Young Children* published by Good Year Books. Copyright © 1997 Shelley Tucker.

Writing Poetry

Tell the children to write or say poems starting with the phrases "dance like," "play like," "paint like," "draw like," and "sing like." They may begin with the same words each time or use different phrases. Review the categories to remind them of the many things they might name.

Making Art

The children then make paper windsocks to illustrate their poems. Give each child a sheet of butcher paper, 4 to 8 feet (approximately 1.2 m to 2.4 m) long, folded in half. Have them draw a large picture on one side of the paper, decorate it, and cut it out in duplicate. Next, ask them to staple the two sheets together, leaving gaps at the tops and bottoms or on the right and left sides of their shapes. An adult then rolls the open edges of their shapes back over pipe cleaners to form openings to catch the wind. Put string on each side of the pipe cleaners, hang up their shapes, and watch the windsocks dance.

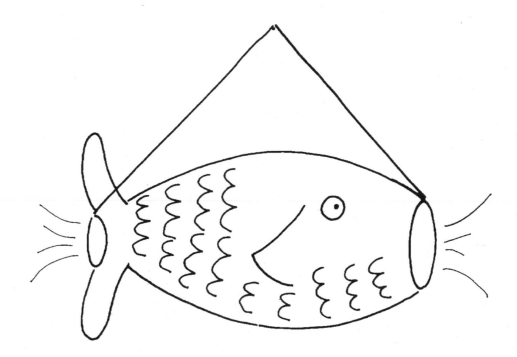

MOVE

Move like the leaves on a tree.

Dream like a shark in the water.

Dance like the fish in the sea.

Sing like a whale in the ocean.

Play like a seal on the Galapagos Islands.

Paul Bruene, age 5

BLUE

Dance like blue,

fast and quick

in the winter.

Harry Howell, age 5

Dance like the tree
as it waves side to side.
Paint like the clouds
as they chase each other.
Sing like spring
as it welcomes you.
Dream like a chipmunk
as it waits for spring to come.

Katelyn Melvey, age 7

SING AND DANCE

Sing like a peacock

cooing at the stars.

Dance like the wind

gliding from the east.

Lucas Powers, age 7

From *Word Weavings: Writing Poetry with Young Children* published by Good Year Books. Copyright © 1997 Shelley Tucker.

Listen to a Tree

Description

Read the phrase "listen to the train," and it is easy to imagine the roar of an engine as it chugs down the tracks. The word *listen* directs us to the sound of the train while the word *train* evokes images of its size, shape, length, color, and speed.

In this exercise, children start lines in their poems with the phrase "listen to" and the word *hear* to engage all of our senses. Then they construct mobiles to make or show the sounds in their poems.

Presentation

Write the following words on the board and review them with the children:

> *listen to   hear*

Tell the children that in poetry, we can write about things we really hear. We may also name things we don't actually hear. Ask them to start with the phrase "listen to" and add the name of something that grows outside.

Examples:
> Listen to a tree.
> Listen to a tomato.

After a few responses, ask the children some of the following questions to show them how to extend their ideas:

> *Where? When? Doing what? Telling you what?*
> *Talking about what? Saying what?*

Example:
> **CHILD:** *Listen to a tree.*
> **TEACHER:** *Telling you what?*
> **SAME OR ANOTHER CHILD:** *About its roots.*
> **TEACHER:** *We can put both parts together and say, "Listen to a tree telling you about its roots."*

Then ask the children to start with the phrase "listen to" and add the name of a color.

Examples:
> Listen to yellow.
> Listen to green.

From *Word Weavings: Writing Poetry with Young Children* published by Good Year Books. Copyright © 1997 Shelley Tucker.

Art Materials

- Pencils, crayons, or markers

- Drawing paper or found objects such as leaves, stones, and shells

- Scissors

- Strong thread or string

- Twigs, branches, or dowels

After a few responses, ask some of the following questions to show them how to extend their ideas.

> *Where? When? Doing what? Telling you what? Saying what?*
> *What does (name the color) talk about?*

Example:

> **CHILD:** *Listen to yellow.*
> **TEACHER:** *What does yellow talk about?*
> **SAME OR ANOTHER CHILD:** *The sun.*
> **TEACHER:** *Who can put both parts together?*
> **CHILD OR TEACHER:** *Listen to yellow talking about the sun.*

(With practice, the children will learn to combine the phrases by themselves.)

Practice

Give the children more practice composing poems that start with the phrase "listen to."

■ List the following categories on the board and choose one:

weather	*animals*	*musical instruments*
machines	*geometric figures*	*things in the sky*

■ Ask the children to start with the phrase "listen to" and add an example from that category.

■ After a few responses, ask some questions to show them how to extend their ideas.

■ Repeat the steps using the word *hear* in place of "listen to."

Writing Poetry

Tell the children to start lines of their poems with the words, *listen to* and *hear.* Remind them of the categories, and review some ways they can extend their ideas.

Making Art

The children construct mobiles to make or show the sounds in their poems. They can use objects they find at home or outdoors, such as pencils, pebbles, or feathers. They might also include pictures that they draw. Have the children put thread through or around their objects and pictures and hang them from dowels, branches, or twigs. For variation, they might place their objects close together so that their mobiles will chime when the wind blows.

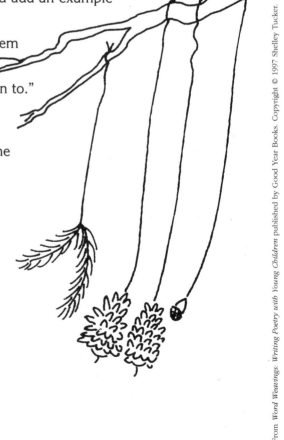

LISTEN

Listen to the kittens purring before their midnight sleep.

Listen to the pony galloping in the meadow.

Hear the water running through the river.

Hear the stars twinkling at night.

Listen to the trees waving.

Listen to the thunder rumbling in the wind.

Michelle Nevins, age 6

Listen to the thunder crackle
as it hits the ground.
Listen to the sunset
as night takes over day.

Aaron Payne, age 5

RAINBOW

Listen to the rainbow's
reflection on the water.
Listen to the abc's
floating in your head.

Aiden Duffy, age 5

Listen to the shark swimming through the ocean.

Listen to the fish shiver.

Hear the fins shining.

Listen to the dolphins swimming in the sea.

ChunMi Araki, age 6

From *Word Weavings: Writing Poetry with Young Children* published by Good Year Books. Copyright © 1997 Shelley Tucker.

Weave the Night

Description

The words *weave, stitch,* and *sew* name actions to create pictures that seem to move in and out like square dancing.

In this exercise, children begin their sentences with the verbs *weave, stitch,* and *sew.* Then they make pictures of their poems and weave through parts of these drawings.

Presentation

Write the following words on the board and review them with the children:

weave	*sew*	*stitch*

Tell them that it is common to write "sew a shirt" or "weave a scarf." In poetry, we may also say different things, such as "weave a day" or "sew some love."

Ask the children to start with the word *weave* and add the name of something in the sky.

Examples:
> *Weave a rainbow.*
> *Weave the stars.*

After a few responses, ask some of the following questions to show them how to extend their ideas:

> *Where? When? Why? How? Using what? With what?*

Example:
> **CHILD:** *Weave a rainbow.*
> **TEACHER:** *With what?*
> **CHILD:** *Colors.*
> **TEACHER:** *We can put both parts together and say, "Weave a rainbow with colors."*

From *Word Weavings: Writing Poetry with Young Children* published by Good Year Books. Copyright © 1997 Shelley Tucker.

Then ask the children to start with the word *weave* and add the name of something that grows outside.

Examples:

> *Weave a rose.*
> *Weave some trees.*

After a few responses, ask some of the following questions to show them how to extend their ideas:

> *Where? When? Why? How? To make what?*

Example:

> **CHILD:** *Weave a rose.*
> **TEACHER:** *Where?*
> **SAME OR ANOTHER CHILD:** *In a garden.*
> **TEACHER:** *Who can put both parts together?*
> **TEACHER OR CHILD:** *Weave a rose in a garden.*

(With practice, children will combine the phrases by themselves.)

Practice

Provide the children with more practice writing poems that start with the word *weave.*

■ List the following categories on the board and choose one:

> *weather*
> *months*
> *feelings*
> *seasons*
> *holidays*
> *things in bodies of water*

■ Have the children start with the word *weave* and then add an example from that category.

■ Ask some of the questions to help them extend their ideas.

■ Then follow the same steps using the words *sew* and *stitch* in place of *weave.*

Writing Poetry

Tell the children to write or say poems, starting their lines with the words *weave, sew,* and *stitch.* Show them the categories to remind them of some of the many things they might name.

Making Art

Have the children draw pictures illustrating their poems. Later, they will weave through parts of their drawings. Pictures that are somewhat symmetrical, such as trees, cats, houses, and people are the easiest to weave.

Ask the children to fold one end of their pictures in half to meet the other end. Make parallel cuts, 1/2 to 1 inch (1.27 to 2.54 cm) apart, across the fold from one edge of the picture to the other. Have the children weave paper strips through the cuts in their papers. Next, ask them to turn their drawings over and put strips of tape across their weavings to secure their work.

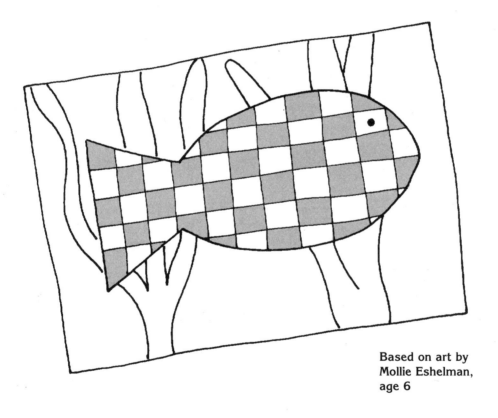

Based on art by
Mollie Eshelman,
age 6

From *Word Weavings: Writing Poetry with Young Children* published by Good Year Books. Copyright © 1997 Shelley Tucker.

FOREST

Weave the forest.

Make the trees and grass grow.

Hear the snake,

rattle, rattle, rattle.

Better hurry up and

paddle, paddle, paddle.

The wind blows in my hair.

When the sun comes out

it will shine on me.

Raymond Leighton, age 6

COLORS OF TIME

Weave a rainbow with colors of time.

Sew the trees against the blackening sky.

Stitch a pattern in the green meadow.

Paint the stars like lemon drops.

Cut the ocean into waves like sand.

Knit a flock of birds on soaring wings.

Eleni Adams, age 10

SEW COLOR

Sew a globe.

Stitch a drawing.

Weave grapes to leaves.

Sew cloth to my house.

Stitch hearts to the fourteenth.

Weave paper in strips.

Sew color.

Alison Haruta, age 6

WEAVE THE SKY

I can sew a cloud of sunshine

that turns like the pages of a book.

I can weave every blade of grass

to the moonlight.

Mollie Price, age 8

Weave a cake in the refrigerator,

a chocolate cake with mint icing.

Sew candles on it

and stitch fire to the candles.

Michelle Nevins, age 5

Dream Like Spaghetti

Description

Sometimes poems are like waking dreams. Unusual comparisons seem sensible, and images offer us new information.

In this exercise, the children start lines of their poems with the words *sleep, dream, wake,* and *rise.* Then they make figures with movable parts that seem to sleep and rise.

From *Word Weavings: Writing Poetry with Young Children* published by Good Year Books. Copyright © 1997 Shelley Tucker.

Presentation

Write the following phrases on the board and review them with the children:

> *sleep like*
> *dream like*
> *wake like*
> *rise like*

Tell them that in poetry we might write "sleep like the boy" or "dream like the girl." Poetry allows us to write more unusual things too. In a poem, we might say "sleep like a lake" or "dream like the moon."

Have the children start with the phrase "sleep like" and then add the name of an animal.

Examples:
> *Sleep like a tiger.*
> *Sleep like an elephant.*

After a few responses, ask some of the following questions to show the children how to extend their ideas:

> *Where? When? Why? How?*

Example:
> **CHILD:** *Sleep like a tiger.*
>
> **TEACHER:** *Where?*
>
> **SAME OR ANOTHER CHILD:** *Under the moonlight.*
>
> **TEACHER:** *We can put both parts together and say, "Sleep like a tiger under the moonlight."*

Art Materials

- Tagboard, pieces of file folders, or other stiff paper

- Pencils, crayons, or markers

- Scissors

- Fasteners that push through paper and open on the other side

- *Optional:* Thin sticks

Then have the children start with the phrase "dream like" and add the name of a color.

Examples:

> Dream like blue.
> Dream like red.

After a few responses, ask the following questions to help the children extend their ideas:

> Where? When? Why? What does (name the color) think about?

Example:

> **CHILD:** Dream like blue.
>
> **TEACHER:** What do you think blue dreams about?
>
> **SAME OR ANOTHER CHILD:** The sky.
>
> **TEACHER:** Who can put both parts together to make one long sentence?
>
> **CHILD OR TEACHER:** Dream like blue thinking about the sky.

(With practice, the children will learn to combine the phrases by themselves.)

Practice

Provide the children with more practice by doing this exercise:

■ List the following categories on the board and choose one:

> weather
> machines
> feelings
> seasons
> months
> sports

■ Have the children start with the phrase "wake like" and add an example from that category.

■ Ask questions to show them ways to extend their ideas.

■ Repeat the steps using the words "rise like" in place of "wake like." Provide as much practice as needed, using both line starts again with different categories.

Writing Poetry

Tell the children to write or say poems that start with "sleep like," "dream like," "wake like," and "rise like." Review the categories to remind them of the many types of things they might name.

Making Art

In poetry, any object can be given parts that move. The children illustrate things from their poems and include movable parts in their pictures. First, ask them to draw animals or objects and cut them out in pieces. If they draw a cat, for example, they cut the body and legs in separate parts. If they draw trees, the children cut the branches apart from the trunks.

Ask them to reattach the pieces of their drawings using paper fasteners. If sticks are available, the children might tape one to the main body of their cutouts and others to the movable parts. Then they can move the shapes with their hands or use the sticks. In motion, things rise. When still, they rest. Even the sun needs to sleep.

Sleep like a whale on the ocean floor.

Dream like a kitten

sleeping sideways in a house.

Sleep like a bay orca

underneath the waves.

Rise like a book

opening with animals inside.

Meaghan McClure, age 7

AUTUMN MIST

Sleep like a tiger

in the moonlight.

Dream like the soft river at night.

Wake like the autumn mist

in the falling falls.

Devon Jarrett-Nomide, age 7

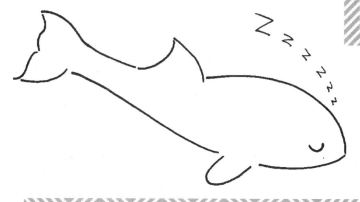

Leap like a tree

dancing in your yard.

Dream like a girl

sleeping in the night.

Wake like a flower

growing in the light.

Caroline Tofflemire, age 6

SLEEP LIKE A KITTEN

Sleep like a kitten

purring by the fire in a chair.

Wake like the raccoon

slipping through the pine forest.

Rise like the ocean

blowing to the shore.

Melissa Chen, age 7

Dinosaur House

From *Word Weavings: Writing Poetry with Young Children* published by Good Year Books. Copyright © 1997 Shelley Tucker.

Art Materials

- Construction paper

- Pencils, crayons, or markers

- Optional: Small tiles, craft sticks, cardboard boxes, Contact® paper, wallpaper, glue

Description

Houses come in all kinds of shapes.

In this exercise, children describe houses using their imaginations to become architects. Then they draw the houses or make three-dimensional models of them.

Presentation

Tell the children that they will be describing make-believe houses. For example, they might write about a rose house, an alligator house, a moon house, or a computer house.

Ask the children to give examples for one of the following types of make-believe houses:

in a forest	*of holidays*	*with animals*
in the sky	*of machines*	*with colors*
of a body of water	*of a month or season*	*with numbers*
of food	*of types of transportation*	*with shapes*
	of things that grow	

Example:

> **TEACHER:** *We can pretend there is a house made of food. For example, I might write about a spaghetti house or a pineapple house. Who will name another pretend house made of food?*
>
> **FIRST CHILD:** *Pizza house.*
>
> **SECOND CHILD:** *Chocolate chip cookie house.*
>
> **THIRD CHILD:** *Ice cream house.*

Choose one of the houses named. Have the children suggest opening sentences for a poem about it. Offer the following line starts if needed:

I have	*In my*	*Have you ever seen a*
My house	*There is*	

Example:

> **TEACHER:** *Who will say a first sentence for a poem about a pizza house?*
>
> **FIRST CHILD:** *Have you ever seen a pizza house?*
>
> **SECOND CHILD:** *There is a pizza house, and you never get hungry in it.*

Then ask the children some of the following questions about the house to help them extend their ideas.

> What does it look like? What is in it? Where is it?
> What happens in it? What do you do in the house?

Example:

TEACHER: *Who will say a sentence about what the pizza house looks like?*

FIRST CHILD: *The pizza house is round and red.*

SECOND CHILD: *Its windows are made of pepperoni.*

THIRD CHILD: *It has eight rooms.*

TEACHER: *Who will tell us a sentence about what you do in a pizza house?*

FIRST CHILD: *You eat pizza all of the time.*

SECOND CHILD: *You run around the outside of the pizza.*

THIRD CHILD: *In my pizza house, everyone is happy.*

Practice

Provide the children with more practice describing imaginary houses.

- Choose a type of house from the list at the beginning of this exercise.
- Have the children give examples of it.
- Then ask questions about the house.

Writing Poetry

Tell the children to write or say poems about their imaginary houses. Review the house categories to remind them of their many choices. Discuss ways they might begin their poems.

Making Art

Have the children construct or draw their houses. If they make three-dimensional models, they might use craft sticks, small pieces of tile, stones, wallpaper, Contact® paper, or cardboard in their constructions. They can also draw their houses on paper and glue on roofs, doors, and windows cut from wallpaper, construction paper, soup labels, or cancelled stamps.

Based on art by Karol Neavor, age 8

ROCK AND ROLL HOUSE

In my rock and roll house,

there is awesome music

and very cool guitars with drums and cymbals.

There are electric pianos with lightning designs

colored red and purple.

In my loud, huge, rock and roll house,

there is good food if you get hungry.

And it's rock and roll goodbye, now.

Dane Hendricksen, age 5

SPOOKY HOUSE

In my spooky house

there is a dinosaur and a dragon.

In my attic there are goblins

that crawl on the floor.

Some fly up high.

Look!

One just locked the door.

Conrad Kluck, age 6

My house is a shiny place

where nothing bad happens.

There are sprinkling gumdrops

and lemonade instead of rain.

Tehut Getahun, age 6

MY WINTER HOUSE

Outside my winter house,

kids are throwing snowballs.

In the ground, trolls are making

flower roots grow.

Down a hole in the ground,

pale sunlight shines

on some bunnies that are asleep.

Max Woodring, age 7

HOUSE UNDERSEA

In my house undersea,

the fish swim in and out.

I like to visit my underwater house

where seaweed goes for grass.

Caitlin Jones-Bamman, age 7

From *Word Weavings: Writing Poetry with Young Children* published by Good Year Books. Copyright © 1997 Shelley Tucker.

Hills Are Shaped Like Bananas

Description

Look at the sky, dig in a garden, or touch a tree, and the clouds, flowers, and leaves whisper poetry.

In this exercise, the children describe natural settings and then make comparisons between them and other objects. Next, they create baskets from paper bags with the tops that show silhouettes of their scenes.

Presentation

Tell the children that they will compose poetry about what they see outside. Ask them to name things they notice at a park, in the sky, at the beach, in the forest, and in a garden. List their suggestions on the board.

Examples:

> children playing baseball
> rain
> flowers
> trees
> vegetables growing
> stars
> people at barbecues
> sky
> dogs running

Choose a topic such as the sky, and ask the children to suggest a first line for a poem about it.

Example:

> **TEACHER:** *Who will suggest a first sentence for a poem about the sky?*
> **CHILD:** *Sometimes I see a rainbow in the sky.*

Tell the children to will select a word from their first sentence and compare it to something else.

Art Materials

- Medium-sized grocery bags with few, if any, markings
- Strips of construction paper
- Pencils, crayons, or markers
- Scissors
- Stapler

Example:

> **TEACHER:** *Now we will choose a word from the sentence and say it is like something else. Let's use the word* rainbow. *We might say, "a rainbow is shaped like a mountain." Who will tell us a sentence about what else a rainbow looks like?*
>
> **FIRST CHILD:** *A rainbow looks like many ice cream flavors.*
>
> **SECOND CHILD:** *Rainbows are in the sky like birds.*
>
> **THIRD CHILD:** *A rainbow looks like an upside-down smile.*

Then review the poem.

Example:

> **TEACHER:** *For our poem, we might say, "Sometimes I see a rainbow. A rainbow looks like many ice cream flavors." We could also say, "Sometimes I see a rainbow. It looks like an upside-down smile."*

Next, have the children suggest a third line for the poem.

Example:

> **TEACHER:** *Who can think of another sentence for this poem?*
>
> **FIRST CHILD:** *Have you ever seen the end of a rainbow?*
>
> **SECOND CHILD:** *Rainbows are high in the sky.*

Repeat the entire poem.

Example:

> **TEACHER:** *There are many ways to write a poem. Here's one:*
>
> > *Sometimes I see a rainbow.*
> > *It looks like an upside-down smile.*
> > *Have you ever seen the end of a rainbow?*
> > *Rainbows are high in the sky.*

Practice

Provide the children with more practice by doing this exercise:

- Select a topic from the board.

- Ask them to suggest first sentences for a poem about it.

- Choose one line for a demonstration. Have the children choose something from it and compare it to another object or action.

- Repeat the steps having the children compose second and third sentences with comparisons.

- Review the entire poem.

From *Word Weavings: Writing Poetry with Young Children* published by Good Year Books. Copyright © 1997 Shelley Tucker.

Writing Poetry

Tell the children to write or say poems about things they see outside. Remind them to describe how something in their poem seems like another object or action.

Making Art

Paper bags make ideal canvases for drawings of nature scenes. The texture of these bags looks like sand, water, and earth.

First, have the children illustrate their poems on paper bags and cut out the tops of their pictures. Next, ask them to decorate the bags and attach strips of paper for handles. Their bags take on the appearance of baskets, textured and curved, and ready to hold stones, leaves, twigs, and acorns.

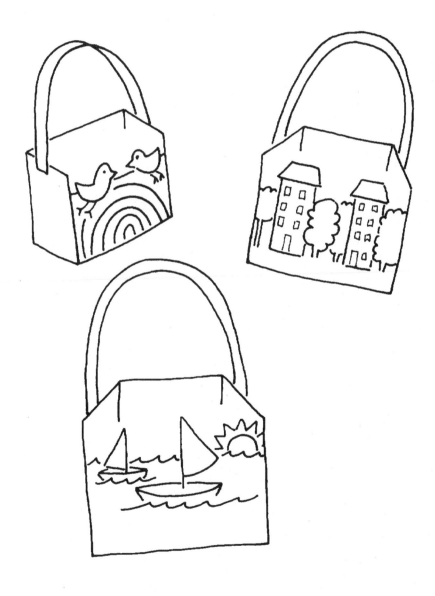

CAMPING

My tent is warm and brown

and smells like fresh air.

It is like a beaver's house.

I like waking up in my red sleeping bag.

We have sausage, eggs, bacon,

and mashed potatoes for breakfast.

I feel good,

like a bear in the morning.

Briana Brewer, age 6

I saw a rainbow bush.

It had all the colors of roses

like a rainbow.

A beautiful flock of birds

flew on it.

Emily Wood, age 5

Boats float with sailors on them.

The sailors are singing

and kicking their legs,

like waves splashing

and roaring in the wind.

Soon night comes.

The sun goes down

and the moon shines

on the water.

Olivia Hoffmeyer, age 7

IN MY YARD

In my backyard,

a rosebush is blooming.

It looks like my mom's camellia bush.

In my front yard, I see a cat.

My cat seems black as thunder.

Taylor Betts, age 5

From *Word Weavings: Writing Poetry with Young Children* published by Good Year Books. Copyright © 1997 Shelley Tucker.

An *inquiry* is a question.

Children often write imaginative poems in response to interesting questions. Consider Casey's answer to the question, "What is in your bottle?"

MAGIC BOTTLE

My bottle is full of magic,

sparklers, swirlers,

and little miniature toys

that tap dance and do ballet.

When I open my bottle,

a rocket shoots out.

I jump on

and sing along.

Casey Ikeda, age 7

Questions and answers are partners. Like two children holding hands, when the first enters a room, the second quickly follows. Ask the children interesting questions, and their responses come almost immediately. Questions about the contents of containers provide rich subjects for children's imaginations.

In the exercises "Bottle of Ideas" and "A Box of Pine Cones," children answer questions about real and imaginary things stored in their containers. "Pocket of Sunlight" and "A Bag of Coral and Shells" combine inquiry with other poetic elements. In "Pocket of Sunlight," the children end their poems by comparing the pocket to something else. In "A Bag of Coral and Shells," they compare things in their bags and other objects.

Through poetry, the children see that containers come in many forms; even poems are houses for words. What better way to open these containers than with keys? The exercise "This Key Unlocks the Galaxy" gives children the opportunity to write about the things that keys start, open, and unlock.

What is in a bottle, box, bag, and pocket? What does a key open or start? Just ask children, and they will readily answer these questions with poetry.

From *Word Weavings: Writing Poetry with Young Children* published by Good Year Books. Copyright © 1997 Shelley Tucker.

Bottle of Ideas

From *Word Weavings: Writing Poetry with Young Children* published by Good Year Books. Copyright © 1997 Shelley Tucker.

Art Materials

- Plastic bottles and lids (Quart bottles from juice or drinking water are ideal because their labels are easy to remove.)

- Glue

- Scissors

- Things to put on bottles: Contact® paper and blank mailing labels cut into shapes, stickers, wrapping paper, ribbon, yarn, aluminum foil, sequins, metallic confetti, drawings, maps

Description

Imagine a bottle with a message in it.

In this exercise, the children experience the adventure of writing poems and putting them in bottles that they decorate.

Presentation

Tell the children that poetry allows us to pretend that bottles might hold unlikely things. For example, we might say that we have a bottle of stars, love, or alligators.

Write the following categories on the board:

things in the sky	*things in the ocean*
holidays	*machines*
feelings	*weather*
countries, states, cities	*sports*

Then choose one. Ask the children to name things from that category that they can pretend are in the bottle.

Example:

> **TEACHER:** *What are some objects in the sky that we can make believe are in this bottle?*
>
> **FIRST CHILD:** *Stars.*
>
> **SECOND CHILD:** *Moon.*
>
> **THIRD CHILD:** *Clouds.*

Work with the children on forming complete sentences for their poems. Ask them ways to begin their lines or suggest the following line starts:

In this bottle	*I have a bottle of*	*In my bottle*	*This bottle*

Example:

> **TEACHER:** *Who will suggest a first sentence for a poem about a bottle full of stars?*
>
> **CHILD:** *In my bottle are bright and shiny stars.*
>
> **TEACHER:** *Who will add a second sentence to this poem about stars in a bottle?*
>
> **SAME OR ANOTHER CHILD:** *When I open the bottle, light pours out.*

Then review the poem with them.

Example:

> *In my bottle
> are bright and shiny stars.
> When I open the bottle,
> light pours out.*

Practice

Give the children more practice doing this exercise:

- Choose a category.

- Have the children name items in the category that they can pretend are in a bottle.

- Choose one of their suggestions and ask them for a first, second, and, possibly, third sentence for a poem about that topic.

- Review the entire poem.

Writing Poetry

Tell the children to write or say poems about bottles that hold imaginary things. Review the categories to show them some of the many things they might name. Discuss ways to start their sentences.

Have the children write their poetry on paper that is slightly shorter than the height of their bottles. Next, ask them to roll up their poems, put rubber bands or ribbons around them, and place the poems in their bottles.

Making Art

Ask children to decorate the bottles to illustrate their poems. Contact® paper and blank mailing labels make ideal materials. After the children draw pictures on them, have them cut out their drawings and stick them on their bottles. Ribbons, yarn, string, bows, and glitter give the bottles additional flair.

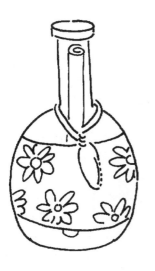

In my bottle,

there is a magic bird

flying over the ocean

with sand and shells

on its wings.

It is whiter than snow,

smoother than silk,

and more colorful than a rainbow.

Alison Haruta, age 7

BLUE JAYS

Have you ever seen a bottle

of blue jays?

They are as blue

as the sky.

Sara Vichorek, age 6

In my bottle

there is joy.

The flowers are blooming

in the summer.

They shine every time

they see you.

Allegra Condiotty, age 5

UFO

In this bottle,

I have a UFO

It blinks on and off,

swerves around, curves

on the Intergalactic Highway,

and zooms past planets,

meteors, and asteroids.

Will Scott, age 8

In my bottle, I have a flying Pegasus.

It is related to horses.

In my bottle, there is a howling coyote

that chases rabbits

into the wild winter.

In my bottle, I have killer whales

flipping and flopping

with the joy of summer

coming to them.

Briar Schwartz, age 6

From *Word Weavings: Writing Poetry with Young Children* published by Good Year Books. Copyright © 1997 Shelley Tucker.

This Key Unlocks the Galaxy

Description

Wondering what a key opens or starts can spark children's creativity. They soon discover that a single key unlocks the imagination.

In this activity, the children describe what keys do. Then they make pictures to illustrate their poems, drawing or including keys in their art.

Presentation

Show the children some keys. Tell them that a key opens an ordinary door or starts a car. In poetry, a key can open the sky, start September, or unlock dreams.

Write the following questions on the board and review them with the children. Then hold up a key. Ask the children to answer one of these questions about it:

> *What does this key open?*
> *What does this key start?*
> *What does this key unlock?*

Have the children begin with the phrase "this key opens" and end with the name of something in the sky.

Examples:
> *This key opens the sun.*
> *This key opens a spaceship.*
> *This key opens a rainbow.*

After a few responses, ask some of the following questions to show the children how to extend their ideas:

> *Where? When? Why? How? What's inside?*

Art Materials

- Drawing paper
- Pencils, crayons, or markers
- Glue
- Keys or paper templates of keys

Example:	**CHILD:** *This key opens the sun.* **TEACHER:** *When?* **SAME OR ANOTHER CHILD:** *In the morning.* **TEACHER:** *We can put both parts together and say, "This key opens the sun in the morning."*

Then ask the children to start with the phrase "this key opens" and name a season:

Examples:	*This key open summer.* *This key opens winter.*

After a few responses, ask some of the following questions to show them how to extend their ideas:

Where? When? Why? How? What happens in (name the season)?

Example:	**CHILD:** *This key opens summer.* **TEACHER:** *What happens in summer?* **SAME OR ANOTHER CHILD:** *We go swimming.* **TEACHER:** *Who can put both parts together?* **CHILD OR TEACHER:** *This key opens summer, and we go swimming.*

(With practice, the children will learn to combine the phrases by themselves.)

Practice

Give them more practice by doing this exercise:

■ Choose one of the following categories:

colors *seasons* *feelings* *things in a forest* *places* *holidays* *months*

■ Have the children begin with the phrase "this key starts" and name something from that category.

■ Ask questions to show them how to extend their ideas.

■ Repeat the steps using the phrase "this key unlocks" in place of "this key starts."

From *Word Weavings: Writing Poetry with Young Children* published by Good Year Books. Copyright © 1997 Shelley Tucker.

Writing Poetry

Tell the students to write or say poems answering one or more of the following questions:

> *What does this key open?*
> *What does this key start?*
> *What does this key unlock?*

Ask or tell them other ways they might begin their poems.

Examples:
> *My key opens/starts/unlocks*
>
> *I have a key and it opens/starts/unlocks*
>
> *Have you ever had a key that opens/starts/unlocks*

Review the categories with the children. Remind them that in poetry, we can pretend that keys open many different things.

Making Art

The keys are the key to this art. Have the children create pictures to illustrate their poems and include actual or drawn keys. They might use the outline of a key for the body of an animal, the trunk of a tree, the frame of a door, or any other shape.

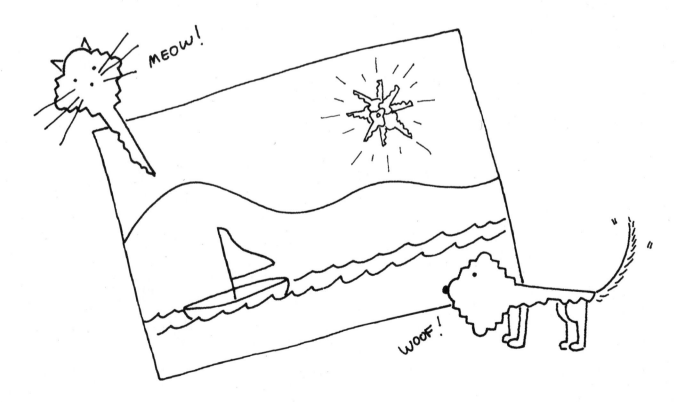

A key opens a cloud of life.

A key opens a rainbow.

This key opens a lot of things.

It opens my heart.

Nighia Nguyen, age 6

JUNGLE

My key can open the day.

My key can unlock the night.

My key opens the wildlife in the jungle.

In the jungle a toucan talks to me.

A lioness nurses its cub

while the others play

while the earth turns around.

Katelyn Melvey, age 7

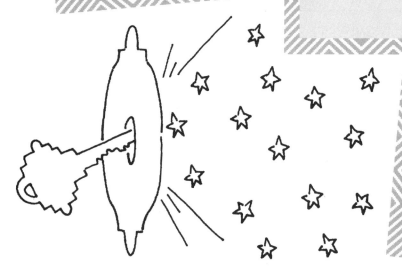

THE KEY TO ME

The key to me

unlocks my brain.

and my thoughts come out.

Nicholas Boroughs, age 7

My key opens the Milky Way.

This key starts the sunbeams.

This key unlocks the light of day

and it's the start

of a space adventure.

Kevin McKenna, age 7

The key of sunlight

opens the sky.

The key of love

unlocks the door of peace.

Tracey Waldman, age 8

From *Word Weavings: Writing Poetry with Young Children* published by Good Year Books. Copyright © 1997 Shelley Tucker.

Pocket of Sunlight

Description

Pockets often contain treasures. A child's pocket might be packed with candy and crayons. Deeper adult pockets have room for coins and keys. Imaginary pockets in the sky hold clouds.

In this exercise, children describe pockets that contain unexpected things. Next, they summarize their ideas, starting the last lines of their poems with the phrase "It is a pocket of." The children decorate their paper or fabric pockets to illustrate their poems.

Presentation

Write the following phrases on the board and then review them with the children:

In my pocket	*I have a pocket of*
In this pocket	*My pocket has*

Ask them to name things that can be found in pockets. Tell them that in poetry, we might write about common objects in pockets, such as keys, gum, and money. Poetry also gives us a way to write about pockets that contain other things too, such as love, flowers, or songs.

Have the children start with one of the phrases on the board and add the name of something in the sky.

Examples:
> *In my pocket is a rainbow.*
> *I have a pocket of clouds and stars.*
> *In this pocket is moonlight.*

Choose one example. Then ask the children to add a related sentence.

Example:
> **TEACHER:** *Let's use, "In my pocket is a rainbow," as the first line of a poem. Who will suggest a sentence that tells us more about a rainbow?*
>
> **CHILD:** *Sometimes I feel like I can touch it.*
>
> **TEACHER:** *The first two sentences of our poem are:*
> > *In my pocket is a rainbow.*
> > *Sometimes I feel like I can touch it.*

From *Word Weavings: Writing Poetry with Young Children* published by Good Year Books. Copyright © 1997 Shelley Tucker.

Write "It is a pocket of" on the board. Show the children how to compose the last lines of their poems starting with that phrase.

Example:

> **TEACHER:** *You will begin the last line of your poems with the words "It is a pocket of." If I have a rainbow in my pocket, I might say that it is a pocket of brightness. What else is a rainbow a pocket of? Add a word that describes the rainbow but is not already in the poem.*
>
> **FIRST CHILD:** *Color.*
>
> **TEACHER:** *What else is a rainbow a pocket of?*
>
> **SECOND CHILD:** *Light.*
>
> **TEACHER:** *What else is a rainbow a pocket of?*
>
> **THIRD CHILD:** *Lines.*
>
> **TEACHER:** *There are many ways we could say this poem. Here's one:*
>
> > *In my pocket is a rainbow.*
> > *Sometimes I feel like I can touch it.*
> > *It is a pocket of color.*

Example including all the steps:

> **TEACHER:** *Who will start with one of these phrases (pointing to the board): "In my pocket," "In this pocket," "I have a pocket of," or "My pocket has," and then name a season?*
>
> **CHILD:** *In my pocket is summer.*
>
> **TEACHER:** *Who will tell us a sentence about summer?*
>
> **SAME OR ANOTHER CHILD:** *In the summer we go swimming.*
>
> **TEACHER:** *Here's our poem so far:*
>
> > *In my pocket is summer.*
> > *In the summer we go swimming.*
>
> *Now who will start with the words, "It is a pocket of," and add a word that describes swimming but is not already in the poem?*
>
> **SAME OR ANOTHER CHILD:** *It is a pocket of splashing.*
>
> **TEACHER:** *What else can we say it is a pocket of?*
>
> **SECOND CHILD:** *It is a pocket of fun.*
>
> **THIRD CHILD:** *It is a pocket of wet bathing suits.*
>
> **TEACHER:** *Here's one way to write this poem:*
>
> > *In my pocket is summer.*
> > *In the summer we go swimming.*
> > *It is a pocket of fun.*

From *Word Weavings: Writing Poetry with Young Children* published by Good Year Books. Copyright © 1997 Shelley Tucker.

Practice

Repeat the steps to give the children practice doing this exercise:

■ Choose a category:

> *seasons*
> *months*
> *things that grow outside*
> *colors*
> *things in the ocean*

■ Have the children start with one of the following phrases and then add the name of something from the category.

> *In my pocket*
> *In this pocket*
> *I have a pocket of*
> *My pocket has*

■ Ask them to suggest another sentence related to the first.

■ Work with the children on the last line of the poem. Have them begin with the phrase "It is a pocket of." Ask them to add a word that describes the subject of their poem but is not already in it.

■ Review the entire poem with them.

Writing Poetry

Tell the children to choose one of the phrases from the board to start their poems and name items not usually found in pockets. Then have them write another related sentence. Have them start the last lines of their poems with the words "It is a pocket of" and add a new word to describe the object in the pocket.

Making Art

Provide the children with pockets made of fabric or paper. For paper pockets, cut 8-1/2 by 11 inch pieces of paper in half. Hold each sheet vertically. Fold up the bottom third of the paper and staple it along the sides to form a pocket. Have the children decorate their pockets and put pictures of things in them to create pockets of art.

In my pocket is a tiger.

My tiger roars.

It is a pocket of danger.

In my pocket there is an octopus.

It has eight legs.

It is a pocket of excitement.

Ryann McChesney, age 6

In my pocket is purple.

It makes a rainbow.

The pocket is full of colors.

In my pocket is the wind.

swift, long, and short.

It is a pocket

full of the blue colored sky.

Osani Shapiro, age 6

IN MY POCKET

In my pocket

shells are clinking

against each other.

They are from the beach.

It is a pocket of water.

In this pocket

there are dolphins

flipping in the sky.

It is a pocket of squealing.

In my pocket

wild horses gallop in the wind.

The hooves sound like drums.

It is a pocket of flying manes.

Briar Schwartz, age 6

In my pocket, I have a jet.

It is roaring up in the sky.

It is a pocket of speed.

Noam Nicholson, age 6

I have a pocket,

and in it there is a black marker.

If you color with it,

you will see the midnight sky.

It is a pocket of moons.

Mollie Esheleman, age 6

A Bag of Pebbles

Description

Ideas for poems come from all kinds of places. They can be found at home, in school, or in parks and then stored in paper bags. Natural objects, such as leaves, twigs, and stones often inspire the poetry with the most interesting ideas and imagery. Just writing the word *leaf* for example, introduces the leaf's size, shape, texture, and color into a poem without ever mentioning these traits.

In this exercise the children answer the question, "What is in my bag?" First they collect small, natural objects and put them in their bags. Then they compose poems about these things and compare them with other objects. They might write, for example, that a feather is like the wind, a twig is shaped like a river, or a stone is round like a penny. The children then decorate their bags to illustrate their poems.

Presentation

Ask the children to show one or two things from their bags to the class. This will help them gather ideas for their poems.

Next, choose an object from a child's bag and then have the children suggest first sentences for a poem about it. Offer the following line starts if needed:

In this bag	I have a bag	In my bag	I put

Example:	**TEACHER:** *Who will suggest a first sentence for a poem about stones?*
	FIRST CHILD: *I found some stones and put them in a bag.*
	SECOND CHILD: *In this bag are stones.*
	THIRD CHILD: *These stones are gray and smooth.*

Then write the following verbs phrases on the board, and review them. These will help the children make comparisons:

looks like	moves like	is shaped like
sounds like	feels like	smells like

Select a verb phrase. Hold up the stones again and tell the children to compare them to other things. For example, they might write "Stones feel like ice." Have the children start with the words "stones feel like" and complete the sentence.

Example:

> **TEACHER:** *Who will start with the words "Stones feel like" and name something else they feel like?*
> **FIRST CHILD:** *Stones feel like glass.*
> **SECOND CHILD:** *Stones feel like hail.*
> **THIRD CHILD:** *Stones feel like bones.*

Choose some of the lines suggested by the children and review the poem.

> **TEACHER:** *There are many ways we could say this poem. Here's one:*
>
> > *In this bag are stones.*
> > *Stones feel like glass.*

Ask the children to add another line to the poem.

Example:

> **TEACHER:** *Who will tell us another sentence for this poem about stones?*
> **FIRST CHILD:** *They come in different colors.*
> **SECOND CHILD:** *Stones remind me of metal.*
> **THIRD CHILD:** *Stones are big and small.*

Add one of their sentences to the poem and review it with them.

Example:

> *In this bag are stones.*
> *Stones feel like glass.*
> *They remind me of metal.*

Practice

Repeat the process many times to give the children practice.

- Choose an object from a bag.
- Ask the children to suggest first sentences for a poem about it.
- Have them compare the object to other things.
- Ask the children to suggest more sentences for the poem.
- Review the entire poem with them.

Writing Poetry

Tell the children to write or say poems about the things in their bags and then compare these objects to other things. Encourage them to use the verbs on the board in their comparisons.

Making Art

Have the children decorate their bags. They might draw pictures, write poems, paste objects, or glue collages on them to create bags of poetry and art.

In my bag, there is a rock
that feels like rough thorns
and smells like the sun.
You can see through the sun
just like glass.

Madeline McCarthy, age 5

In my bag, there is an oyster shell
that looks like a duck.
It has a hole that looks like an eye.
You could wear it as a necklace.

In my bag is a dead flower.
It used to be pretty,
but now it looks like a spiked fish.

In my bag are some stuffed bears.
They have homes at my house.

Briana Brewer, age 6

THE SEA

I have a shell in my bag.
It is like the wind blowing in the ocean.
I have sea glass in my bag.
It is like a seagull fluttering in the air.

Taylor Betts, age 6

FLOWERS AND LEAVES

In my bag are flowers and leaves.
Leaves feel like soft blankets
covering me.
Flowers feel like pillows
under my head.

Kara Kathleen Schuman, age 5

WHAT'S IN MY BAG?

The leaves are like the rainbow.
The branches are like trees
in my backyard.
The shells are from snails on the beach.

Ben Wenet, age 5

Metaphor

A *metaphor* compares two unlike nouns. It is similar to a simile but it makes the connection without the word *like* or *as*.

NIGHT AND DAY

Night is an owl in a bed.

Day is a fish

picked up by a seagull.

The moon is a bird

asleep in the sky.

Patricia Wreford-Brown, age 6

Metaphors do not require large words, so they are easy for children to write. Rather, the power of metaphors comes from the nouns that children select to compare. Consider the following metaphor by Aiyana Hayes:

The sky is the home to the wind.

Her central metaphor, "The sky is the home," is made with two very familiar nouns, *sky* and *home*. Aiyana wrote an interesting metaphor because she chose to connect these nouns. Then she extended her comparison by answering the question, "To what?"

The sky is the home (to what?) *the wind.*

Young children can easily compose metaphors by connecting any two dissimilar nouns with the words *is* or *of*. In the first and last exercises of this chapter, "The Moon Is a Cat" and "Open a Poem," children use the word *is* to make the comparisons. In all of the other models, they connect their nouns with the word *of*. Comparisons of unrelated nouns in metaphors usually create imaginative poetry and can broaden the ways children think about and use language.

From *Word Weavings: Writing Poetry with Young Children* published by Good Year Books. Copyright © 1997 Shelley Tucker.

The Moon Is a Cat

Description

Consider the sentence, "Thunder is an elephant." The characteristics of thunder and the elephant combine to create thick, broad, powerful images and loud, booming sounds.

In this exercise, children compare the moon, lightning, thunder, day, and night to animals. Then they illustrate their poems with pop-up art.

Presentation

Write the following phrases on the board and then review them with the children:

> *The moon is a*
> *Lightning is a*
> *Thunder is a*
> *Day is a*
> *Night is a*

Tell them that in poetry, we might say lightning is weather. Poetry also lets us write more unusual things. For example, we might compare the moon, lightning, thunder, day, and night to animals.

Ask the children to start with the phrase "the moon is" and add the name of an animal that in some way reminds them of the moon.

Examples:
> *The moon is a mouse.*
> *The moon is a cat.*

After a few responses, ask some of the following questions to show the children how to extend their ideas:

> *Where? When? Why? Doing what? How are they alike?*

From *Word Weavings: Writing Poetry with Young Children* published by Good Year Books. Copyright © 1997 Shelley Tucker.

Art Materials

- Construction paper, 2 pieces per child

- Pencils, crayons, or markers

- Scissors

- Glue

Example:

> **CHILD:** *The moon is a mouse.*
> **TEACHER:** *Doing what?*
> **SAME OR ANOTHER CHILD:** *Sleeping.*
> **TEACHER:** *We can put these together and say, "The moon is a mouse sleeping."*

Then ask the children to begin with the phrase "lightning is" and add the name of an animal that in some way reminds them of lightning.

Examples:

> *Lightning is a yellow bird.*
> *Lightning is an eel.*

After a few responses, ask the following questions to help the children extend their ideas:

> *Where? When? Why? Doing what? How are they alike?*

Example:

> **CHILD:** *Lightning is a yellow bird.*
> **TEACHER:** *Where?*
> **SAME OR ANOTHER CHILD:** *In the sky.*
> **TEACHER:** *Who can put both parts together?*
> **CHILD OR TEACHER:** *Lightning is a yellow bird in the sky.*

(After some practice, children wil combine the phrases by themselves.)

Practice

Repeat the same process for each of the line starts, "thunder is," "day is," and "night is."

- Choose a line start.

- Have the children begin with it, and then add names of animals that in some way remind them of it.

- Ask questions to show them ways to extend their ideas.

> *Where? When? Why? Doing what? How are they alike?*

Writing Poetry

Reread the five phrases with the children:

> *The moon is a*
> *Lightning is a*
> *Thunder is a*
> *Day is a*
> *Night is a*

Tell them to write or say poems beginning with these words. They may choose which phrases to use and in what order. Have them add the names of animals and make their sentences longer.

Making Art

The children create pop-up art to illustrate their poems. First, ask them to fold a piece of construction paper in half. Next, have them make two parallel cuts across the fold, two inches long each and one inch apart, and fold the tab over at the end of their cuts. Ask them to open their paper and push the tab through to create a stand for the pop-up art. Then, they cut more tabs.

On other sheets of papers, ask the children to draw animals from their poems, showing the characteristics of the moon, lightning, thunder, day, and night in them. Have them cut out these animals and glue them onto the bottom halves of the tabs. When they open their papers, the animals will rise off the pages.

Based on art by Katelyn Melvey, age 7

The moon is a spider

climbing up a web.

Lightning is a rat

when it flashes at night.

Thunder is an earthquake

when the sun comes up.

Day is a storm

with a streak of light.

Night is a cat

running into the street

under a full moon.

Jeremy Kohlenberg, age 5

Thunder is a lion

because they're both stormy.

Lightning is a tiger,

really sharp.

Night is a lynx.

It can see through a stone wall.

Caitlin Wilson, age 6

DAY IS A ZEBRA

Day is a zebra galloping.

Lightning is a giraffe running.

Thunder is a foot stomping.

Night is a cat

creeping across the kitchen.

Elizabeth McDanold, age 8

The night is a shark

in a deep, deep aquarium.

Thunder is a dragon

crashed into the lightning snake.

Timothy Anderson, age 5

From *Word Weavings: Writing Poetry with Young Children* published by Good Year Books. Copyright © 1997 Shelley Tucker.

Song of a Tiger

Description

Listen carefully. Everything has a song. The trees harmonize with the wind. The sun sings counterpoint with the moon. Computers and keyboards do duets.

In this exercise, children use the phrases "song of," "music of," and "notes of" in their poems. Then they make paper-bag puppets that seem to open in song.

Presentation

Write the following words on the board and review them with the children:

song of   music of   notes of

Tell them that in poetry, we might write about songs of happiness and music of friendship. Poetry also allows us to describe more unusual sounds. For example, we might write about the song of the sky, the music of a baseball, or the notes of spring.

Ask the children to start with the phrase "song of" and then add the name of an animal.

Examples: Song of the bear
Song of the turtle

After a few responses, ask some of the following questions to show the children how to extend their ideas:

Is where? Sounds like what? Does what? Says what?

Example:

CHILD: *Song of the bear.*

TEACHER: *Does what?*

SAME OR ANOTHER CHILD: *Hibernates for the winter.*

TEACHER: *We can put both parts together and say, "Song of the bear hibernates for the winter."*

Next, ask the children to start with the phrase "song of" and add the name of a machine.

Examples:

> *song of the refrigerator*
> *song of the computer*

After a few responses, ask some of the following questions to help them extend their ideas:

> *Is where? Sounds like what? Does what? Says what?*

Example:

> **CHILD:** *Song of the refrigerator.*
> **TEACHER:** *Sounds like what?*
> **SAME OR ANOTHER CHILD:** *Crunchy peanut butter.*
> **TEACHER:** *Who can put both parts together?*
> **CHILD OR TEACHER:** *Song of the refrigerator sound like crunchy peanut butter.*

(With practice, children will learn to combine phrases by themselves.)

Practice

For practice, follow these steps using the phrase "music of."

■ Choose one of the these categories:

> *machines*
> *months*
> *numbers*
> *shapes*
> *things that grow outside*
> *things in the sky*
> *weather*
> *seasons*
> *sports*

■ Have the children start with the phrase "music of" and add an example from that category.

■ Ask some of the following questions to show them how to extend their ideas:

> *Is where? Sounds like what? Does what? Says what?*

■ Repeat the steps with the phrase "notes of" instead of "music of."

Writing Poetry

Tell the children to write or say poems using the phrases "song of," "music of," and "notes of." Review the categories with them. For variety, ask them about other ways they might start their poems.

Making Art

Give the children paper bags to make puppets. If a poem is about an animal, the crease in the bag becomes the mouth. The folded part of the bag can also represent a door, a window, clouds, wind, or anything else that moves. Have the children decorate their bags to illustrate their poems. Then they can move the folded parts of their bags as if to open them in song.

Song of the bird
sounds like a flute.
Music of a deer
sounds like the forest.
Notes of spring
sound like the ocean
crashing against the rocks.

Laura Bogar, age 5

MUSIC

Notes of a plane in the air
fly to a city and land.
Music of blue jumps into a pool.
Song of a square feels bumpy.

Noah Baker, age 5

Notes of a jet
cruise down the highway.
Song of the birds
chirp in the sky.
Music of the wind
whispers to you.

Noam Nicholson, age 6

Song of a whale in the sea
looks like a puffy cloud.
Notes of the sky are as blue
as the sun is yellow.
Music of the clouds
with a secret door
does the dances of the sky.

Natalie Hoyt, age 6

SONGS OF ANIMALS

Song of a dog singing at a dance
makes me happy.
Music of a horse running
sounds like trolloping.
Notes of a cat are in the air.

Sara Vichorek, age 5

Garden of Poetry

Description

Gardens and poems have a lot in common. They start with seeds and grow into a bounty for the senses.

In this exercise, the children use the phrases "garden of" and "harvest of" in their poems. Then they construct three-dimensional paper gardens in the lids of shoe boxes to illustrate their poems.

Presentation

Write the following words on the board and then review them with the children:

> *garden of   harvest of*

Tell them that in poetry, we might write about objects we usually see in gardens, such as roses and zucchinis. Poetry also allows us to describe unexpected things, such as a garden of stars or a harvest of happiness.

Ask the children to start with the phrase "garden of" and name a feeling.

Examples:
> *garden of love*
> *garden of surprise*

After a few responses, ask some of the following questions to show them how to extend their ideas:

> *Looks like what? Does what? Grows what?*

Example:

> **CHILD:** *Garden of love.*
>
> **TEACHER:** *Grows what?*
>
> **SAME OR ANOTHER CHILD:** *Flowers shaped like hearts.*
>
> **TEACHER:** *We can put these together and say, "Garden of love grows flowers shaped like hearts."*

Now ask the children to start with the phrase "garden of" and then name a color.

Examples:
> *garden of blue*
> *garden of red*

After a few responses, ask the children some of the following questions to show them how to extend their ideas:

Looks like what? Does what? Grows what?

Example:

CHILD: *Garden of blue.*
TEACHER: *Looks like what?*
SAME OR ANOTHER CHILD: *The sky.*
TEACHER: *Who can put both parts together?*
CHILD OR TEACHER: *Garden of blue looks like the sky.*

(After some practice, the children will learn to combine the phrases by themselves.)

Practice

Provide the children with more practice by using this exercise:

■ Select one of the following categories.

sky   sea   animals   weather

■ Have them start with the phrase "harvest of" and add an example from that category.

■ After a few responses, ask the children questions to help them expand their ideas.

■ Then repeat the steps using the phrase "harvest of" in place of "garden of."

Writing Poetry

Tell the children that they will write or say poems that use the phrases "garden of" and "harvest of." Review the categories to remind them of the many kinds of things they might name.

For variety, ask the children to suggest additional ways to begin their poems. Some other line starts are:

I saw a garden of / harvest of
Have you ever seen a garden of / harvest of
There is a garden of / harvest of

Making Art

Ask the children to add color to their shoe box lids with green markers, crayons, or construction paper. Have them place triangles or spears of green paper around the outside rims of the lids to create grass. Next, ask them to tape the bottom halves of the cardboard strips onto the insides of the shoe box lids, so the top halves of cardboard stick up in the air.

On the pieces of tagboard, tell the children to draw pictures of the things they named in their poems and cut them out. Finally, have them tape their drawings onto the cardboard strips, so the pictures stand up. Through poetry and art, the children expand the edges of the garden to include a harvest of clouds, friends, and stars.

From *Word Weavings: Writing Poetry with Young Children* published by Good Year Books. Copyright © 1997 Shelley Tucker.

Harvest of a slippery fish

sliding through the water.

Harvest of a garden snake

eating the bugs off the leaves.

Timothy Anderson, age 5

Garden of the sun, pretty and bright.

Harvest of purple

squishing and big in the sky,

Garden of the trees

hard and tall on the earth.

Harry Howell, age 5

I harvest the storms of the world

and the garden of colors

and languages.

I harvest happiness.

Brendan McGarry, age 8

POETRY

Garden of feelings,

love and confidence.

I harvest the grains of poetry.

Sarah Petrulis, age 7

HORSES

I have a garden of horses,

saddles, and bridles.

I pick one every day.

I have to find a garden of blankets

or else my horse will get cold.

Emma Fuller, age 7

Quilt of Clouds

From *Word Weavings: Writing Poetry with Young Children* published by Good Year Books. Copyright © 1997 Shelley Tucker.

Art Materials

- 4-inch (approximately 10 cm) squares of tissue paper in warm colors—yellow, orange, and red

- Optional: 4-inch (approximately 10 cm) squares of tissue paper in cool colors—green, blue, and purple

- Mixture of half glue and half water

- Strips of sponges, 1 by 3 inches (2.54 by 7.62 cm) each, to apply the glue

- Scissors

- White construction paper, 12 by 18 inches (approximately 30 by 45 cm), 1 per child for tapestry, 2 per child for weaving

- *Optional:* plastic sticks or branches

Description

Some words immediately engage our senses. The word *quilt* evokes thick, sewn patches of comfort. *Weaving* brings images of materials that go in and out like square dancers. *Tapestry* conjures up wall hangings with golden threads.

In this exercise, the children write poetry that draws on the richness of the words *quilt, weaving,* and *tapestry.* Then they create tissue paper tapestries or weavings to hold their poems.

Presentation

Write the following words on the board and then review them with the children:

> quilt of   weaving of

Tell them that in poetry, we might write about a quilt of fine cotton or a weaving of straw. Poetry gives us a way to write about other things too, for example, "a quilt of love" or "a weaving of rain."

Ask the children to start with the phrase "quilt of" and then name something in the sky.

Examples:
> quilt of clouds
> quilt of stars

Then ask the question, "Does what?" This will show the children how to form sentences by adding a verb.

Example:
> **CHILD:** *Quilt of clouds.*
>
> **TEACHER:** *Does what?*
>
> **SAME OR ANOTHER CHILD:** *Covers the sky.*
>
> **TEACHER:** *We can put it all together and say, "Quilt of clouds covers the sky."*

Next, have the children start with the phrase "quilt of" and name a feeling.

Example:

> *quilt of hope*
> *quilt of love*

Then ask them the question, "Does what?"

Example:

> **CHILD:** *Quilt of hope.*
> **TEACHER:** *Does what?*
> **SAME OR ANOTHER CHILD:** *Keeps me warm.*
> **TEACHER:** *Who will put both parts together?*
> **CHILD OR TEACHER:** *Quilt of hope keeps me warm.*

(With practice, children will combine the phrases by themselves.)

Practice

Give the children practice by doing this exercise:

- Write the following categories on the board, and choose one:

> *things that grow outside*
> *weather*
> *seasons*
> *months*
> *objects in the ocean*

- Have the children start with the phrase "quilt of" and name an example from that category.

- Then ask them the question, "Does what?"

- Repeat the steps using the phrase "weaving of" in place of "quilt of." *(Optional: Use the phrase "tapestry of.")*

Writing Poetry

Tell the children to write or say poems that start with the phrases "quilt of," "weaving of," and "tapestry of." Review the categories to remind them of many things they might name.

Making Art

This art project can be done two ways. One is easy. The other, though more difficult, yields exceptionally beautiful results.

Using the easy method, children create a tapestry of colors on which they can mount their poems. Give each child a sheet of white construction paper, a container with an inch mixture of equal parts of water and glue, a sponge strip, and enough squares of tissue paper in warm colors to cover the sheet of construction paper completely.

Have the children dip their sponges into the glue and moisten one side of their construction paper with it. Next, ask them to lay the tissue on the construction paper. The squares of tissue paper can overlap, wrinkle, or hang off the edges of the construction paper, but they need to cover it completely. After the children apply the tissue paper, have them add a final coat of glue. When it dries, you or the children can trim the excess tissue off the edges of the construction paper. *(Optional: The children fringe the bottom of the construction paper, and you roll the top of the paper around a stick or branch so that it can hang like a tapestry.)*

For a more complex project that involves weaving, have the children first complete the tissue gluing process described above. Then ask them to repeat the steps, pasting tissue paper in cool colors onto another sheet of white construction paper. After it dries, you or the children can trim off the excess tissue paper.

You or another adult then prepare the papers for weaving. First, fold the construction paper with the cool tissue paper in half. Then cut wavy lines, one inch apart, from the fold to two inches from the top of the paper. Next, cut the construction paper covered with warm tissue piece into 1-inch strips. The children then weave the warm-colored strips through the cool sheet. *(Optional: Have the children fringe the bottom of the paper, and you roll the top of it over a stick or branch.)* The children can now glue their poems onto the back of this rainbow-colored weaving.

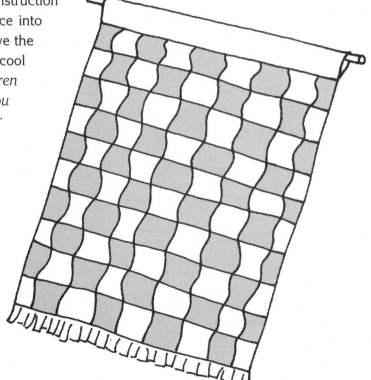

From *Word Weavings: Writing Poetry with Young Children* published by Good Year Books. Copyright © 1997 Shelley Tucker.

Quilts of the plants

grow in the ground.

Tapestry of flowers

have bees in summer.

Weavings of blue jays

fly in the sky.

Briana du Nann, age 7

Blanket of fish swimming in a school

fast through the water

makes the shark tempted

to have a feast.

Montana Tippett, age 8

FOREST

Tapestry of the trees

holds the forest spirit.

Quilt of the fox

pounces on its prey.

Blanket of the owl

swoops silently through the night.

Conrad Kluck, age 6

Tapestry of the ocean

swims around all day.

Blanket of the sun

heats up the earth.

David Price, age 7

Blanket of the starfish

sticks to me hard.

Tosten Haugerud, age 7

From *Word Weavings: Writing Poetry with Young Children* published by Good Year Books. Copyright © 1997 Shelley Tucker.

Bridge of Butterflies

Art Materials

- Cardboard, tagboard, or other heavy paper

- Pencils, crayons, or markers

- Craft sticks, toothpicks, clothespins, small tiles

- Glue

Description

Bridges, roads, and maps point the way to travel and discovery.

In this exercise, children write poetry including the phrases "bridge of," "road of," and "map of." Then, using craft sticks, toothpicks, clothespins, or small tiles, they illustrate their poems.

Presentation

Write the following words on the board and then review them with the children:

bridge of	*road of*	*map of*	.

Tell them that we commonly hear about "a bridge of steel," "a road of concrete," and "a map of the world." In poetry, we may also write about different things, such as "a bridge of peace," "a map of red," or "a road of frogs."

Ask the children to start with the phrase "bridge of" and then add the name of an animal.

Examples:

> *bridge of birds*
> *bridge of wolves*

After a few examples, ask some of the following questions to show them how to extend their ideas:

> *Is where? Does what? Looks like what?*

Example:

> **CHILD:** *Bridge of grasshoppers.*
> **TEACHER:** *Does what?*
> **SAME OR ANOTHER CHILD:** *Stretches across the field.*
> **TEACHER:** *We can put these together and say,*
> *"Bridge of grasshoppers stretches across the field."*

Then have the children begin with the phrase "bridge of" and add the name of something in the sky. After a few examples, ask some of the following questions to help them lengthen their ideas.

> *Is where? Does what? Looks like what?*

From *Word Weavings: Writing Poetry with Young Children* published by Good Year Books. Copyright © 1997 Shelley Tucker.

Example:	**CHILD:** *Bridge of stars.*
	TEACHER: *Looks like what?*
	SAME OR ANOTHER CHILD: *The sun.*
	TEACHER: *Who will put both parts together?*
	CHILD OR TEACHER: *Bridge of stars looks like the sun.*

(After some practice, the children will learn to combine the phrases by themselves.)

Practice

Do the following exercise using the phrase "road of."

■ Choose one of the following categories:

feelings	*things that grow in a forest*	*seasons*
holidays	*fruits and vegetables*	*transportation*
months		

■ Ask the children to start with the phrase "road of" and add an example from the category.

■ After a few responses, ask questions to show the children how to extend their ideas.

■ Then repeat the steps using the phrase "map of" instead of "road of."

Writing Poetry

Tell the children that they will write or say poems using the words "bridge of," "road of," and "map of." Review the categories with them to remind them of the different things they might name.

For variation, ask the children for other ways to start their poems or suggest:

I see	*I saw*	*There is*	*Where is*	*Have you ever seen*

Examples:	*I saw a map of noodles on my plate.*
	There is a bridge of air that connects all people.
	Have you ever seen a road of red going through a rainbow?

Making Art

Ask the children to construct bridges, roads, or maps on paper to illustrate their poems. They might use craft sticks, small tiles, nuts and bolts, toothpicks, clothespins, macaroni, or cardboard to map their creativity.

I see a map of a dog
on a bridge of clouds
that's connected
to the road of summer.

Montana Tippett, age 8

Road of the dinosaurs past,

long through legends.

Bridge in the fog

to a place you have never been.

Map of the mountains

in the clouds.

Jarrett Cordell, age 7

BRIDGE OF BEES

I looked in the sky
and saw a bridge of bees.
Under it were dogs.
The bees were buzzing
with the fireflies.

Luke Theofelus, age 5

ROAD OF GLASS

I see a road

made of clear, smooth glass.

Let me weave in the color.

Lucas Powers, age 7

Map of the past

shining from the sun.

Map of the antelope

leaping for shelter.

Noam Nicholson, age 6

Texture of Popcorn

Description

Poetry is all about texture. Words create layers of pictures and sounds. Sentences weave fabrics of meaning.

In this exercise, the children write about the textures of feelings, colors, animals, sounds, and things. Then they make textured puzzles to illustrate their poems.

Presentation

Write the following phrase on the board and review it with the children:

> *texture of*

Tell them that in poetry, we can talk about the texture of silk or the feel of a leaf. We might also discuss unusual textures, such as that of a storm or the night.

Ask the children to start with the phrase "texture of" and add the name of something that grows outside.

Examples:
> *texture of grass*
> *texture of a rose*
> *texture of bark*

Then ask them to begin with the phrase "texture of" and add the name of a color.

Examples:
> *texture of red*
> *texture of silver*

After a few responses, ask some of the following questions to show them how to extend their ideas:

> *Is where? Feels like what? Looks like what?*

Example:
> **CHILD:** *Texture of red.*
>
> **TEACHER:** *Feels like what?*
>
> **SAME OR ANOTHER CHILD:** *Strawberries and tomatoes.*
>
> **TEACHER:** *We can put it all together and say,*
> *"Texture of red feels like strawberries and tomatoes."*

From *Word Weavings: Writing Poetry with Young Children* published by Good Year Books. Copyright © 1997 Shelley Tucker.

Art Materials

- Tagboard

- Pencils, crayons, or markers

- Glue

- Things to create textured art, such as pasta, sandpaper, cotton balls, sand, paper, stones, rocks, glitter, Contact® paper, aluminum foil

Practice

Give the children more practice using the phrase "texture of."

■ Write some of the following categories on the board:

machines	*shapes*	*weather*
sounds	*animals*	*months*
numbers	*times of day*	*things in the sky*
sports		

■ Select a category. Then have the children start with the phrase "texture of" and add an example from that category.

■ After a couple of responses, ask some of the following questions to show the children how to extend their ideas:

> *Is where? Feels like what? Looks like what?*

(With practice, the children will combine the phrases independently.)

Writing Poetry

Tell the children to write or say poems using the phrase "texture of." Review the list of categories to remind them of the different things they might name in their poems.

For variety, ask the children for other ways they can start their poems or suggest the following:

Examples:
> *Have you ever felt the texture of*
> *I saw the texture of*
> *What is the texture of*

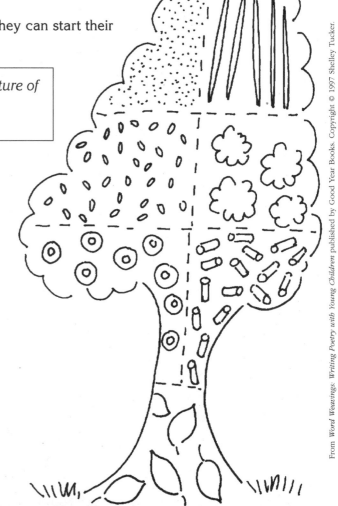

Making Art

Give each child a piece of tagboard. Have the children draw a picture of something from their poems and cut it into pieces to form a puzzle. Then they can glue things with different textures, such as cotton, toothpicks, pasta, beans, hardware, sandpaper, rocks, dirt, sand, stones, and leaves, onto each piece of their puzzles.

From *Word Weavings: Writing Poetry with Young Children* published by Good Year Books. Copyright © 1997 Shelley Tucker.

Did you ever see the texture

of a white cloud

against the blue sky?

Have you ever seen the texture

of a zebra's black stripes

against its white coat?

Elise Burnett, age 7

TEXTURE OF EARTH

I see the texture

of the mighty tree.

The texture of the earth

is the core of it.

Asa Trapp, age 7

DRAGON

The texture of a dragon
is in its tail.

Conrad Kluck, age 6

TEXTURE OF LIFE

I see, feel, want, and need

the texture of life.

It's soft like the moon,

the sun, the clouds,

and my blanket

that keeps me warm at night.

Stephanie Loomis, age 7

The texture of dew

on the blossoming bud

of a springtime rose

is like the smell

of the rainbow in the sky.

Karol Neavor, age 8

From *Word Weavings: Writing Poetry with Young Children* published by Good Year Books. Copyright © 1997 Shelley Tucker.

Design of Porcupines

From *Word Weavings: Writing Poetry with Young Children* published by Good Year Books. Copyright © 1997 Shelley Tucker.

Art Materials

- Construction paper

- Pencils, crayons, or markers

- Things to create designs and patterns: tissue paper, uncooked pasta, soup labels, ribbons, beans, canceled stamps, ribbon, pieces of wrapping paper

Description

Children compose poems to show the design of their observations, thoughts, and feelings with words.

In this exercise, they use the phrases "design of," "pattern of," and "mosaic of." Then they make designs and patterns to illustrate their poems.

Presentation

Write the following words on the board, and then review them with the children:

design of	pattern of	mosaic of

Then tell them that we expect to hear about designs on paper and patterns on clothes. In poetry, we might also celebrate a design of tomatoes in the market or a pattern of clouds in the sky.

Ask the children to begin with the phrase "design of" and then name something that grows in a forest, park, or garden.

Examples:
> design of daisies
> design of trees
> design of bark

After a few responses, ask some of the following questions to show the children how to extend their ideas:

> Does what?
> Feels like what?
> Reminds you of what?
> Looks like what?

Example:
> **CHILD:** *Design of daisies.*
> **TEACHER:** *Looks like what?*
> **SAME OR ANOTHER CHILD:** *The sun.*
> **TEACHER:** *We can put these together and say,
> "Design of daisies looks like the sun."*

Then ask the children to begin with the phrase "design of" and add the name of some kind of weather.

Examples:

> *design of snow*
> *design of tornadoes*

After a few responses, ask the children some of the following questions to help them lengthen their ideas:

> *Does what?*
> *Feels like what?*
> *Reminds you of what?*
> *Looks like what?*

Example:

> **CHILD**: *Design of snow.*
> **TEACHER**: *Does what?*
> **SAME OR ANOTHER CHILD**: *Falls in the meadow.*
> **TEACHER**: *Who will put both parts together?*
> **CHILD OR TEACHER**: *Design of snow falls in the meadow.*

(With practice, the children will learn to combine the phrases by themselves.)

Practice

Provide the children with more practice by doing this exercise:

■ Write the following categories on the board and choose one:

> *colors*
> *food in a grocery store*
> *things in the sky*
> *things in the sea*
> *animals*
> *dwellings*
> *jobs*

■ Have the children start with the words "design of," and add an example from the category.

■ After a few responses, ask questions to show them ways to extend their ideas.

■ Repeat the steps using the phrase "pattern of."
   Optional: Use the phrase "mosaic of."

Writing Poetry

Tell the children to write or say poems with the phrases "design of," "pattern of," and "mosaic of." Review the categories to show them some of the many things they might name.

Have the children begin their lines with the phrases "design of," "pattern of," and "mosaic of," or for variation, suggest that they start with the following words. These beginnings will give them complete sentences:

> *I saw*
> *I see*
> *Have you*
> *There is*

Making Art

Using uncooked pasta, beans, sticks, ribbons, canceled stamps, cut paper, labels, or photographs along with crayons, paint, and markers, have the children create textured designs, patterns, and mosaics. Their pictures might be abstract or realistic.

I saw a pattern of the trees
blowing in the wind,
a design of fish
growing in the sea,
a mosaic of seaweed rolling
on the water of the ocean,
a design of animals
running in the forest,
and a pattern of the wolves
howling at the moon.

Michelle Nevins, age 6

I eat a mosaic of meatballs
from my plate.

Samaya Blaney, age 6

MOSAIC OF TREES

A mosaic of trees
dots the hills
waiting for a person
to hug them.

Sarah Petrulis, age 7

A design in the wind
is like a turtle on an island.

A design on the ocean
is like a great white shark

Rory Voie, age 5

VOLCANO

A design of smooth glass
under dancing waves.
A mosaic of rock
melting in lava
deep in the depths
of the volcano.

Sara Qualin, age 8

Signature of the Whale

Art Materials

- Pencils, crayons, or markers

- 8-1/2 by 11 inch (21.59 by 27.94 cm) or 8-1/2 by 14 inch (21.59 by 35.59 cm) paper with a grid formed of horizontal lines every half inch and vertical lines every 2 inches (5.08 cm), one sheet per child

Description

What if the wind could sign its name? Where would it be, and what would it look like?

This exercise draws on children's interest in printing and writing names. The children use the phrases "signature of" and "handwriting of" to describe animals and things. Then they draw pictures incorporating their names into their designs.

Presentation

Write the following words on the board and review them with the children:

handwriting of   signature of

Tell them that we might write a poem about someone's handwriting or signature. We might also imagine that other things have signatures too. For example, we could say that the handwriting of a snake slithers through a field or the signature of the cloud glides in the sky.

Ask the children to start with the phrase "handwriting of" and name some kind of animal.

Examples:

handwriting of a rabbit
handwriting of a zebra

Then ask some of the following questions to show them how to extend their ideas:

Looks like what? Does what?

Example:

CHILD: *Handwriting of a rabbit.*
TEACHER: *Does what?*
SAME OR ANOTHER CHILD: *Hops.*
TEACHER: *We can put both parts together and say, "The handwriting of a rabbit hops."*

For variety, ask some of the following questions to show the children how to further extend their sentences:

Where? When? Why? How?

> *Example:*
>
> **TEACHER:** *Who will start with the words, "The handwriting of a rabbit hops," and say where it hops?*
>
> **CHILD:** *The handwriting of a rabbit hops through a field.*

Practice

Give the children more practice by doing this exercise:

■ Choose one of the following categories:

> *things that grow outside*   *weather*
> *food*   *objects in the sky*

■ Have the children start with the phrase "handwriting of" and then name an object from the category.

■ Ask some of the following questions to help them form complete sentences:

> *Looks like what? Does what?*

■ Then ask other questions to show the children ways to further lengthen their lines:

> *Where? When? Why? How?*

■ Repeat the steps using the phrase "signature of."

Writing Poetry

Tell the children to write or say poems describing the signatures and handwriting of animals, weather, and anything else except for people. Write the following questions on the board to help the children compose complete sentences:

> *Looks like what? Does what?*

Making Art

Start with a piece of paper measuring 8-1/2 by 11 inches (21.59 by 27.94 cm) or 8-1/2 by 14 inches (21.59 by 35.59 cm). Draw a grid with horizontal lines every half inch and vertical lines every two inches to create a sheet of rectangles. Make a copy of the grid for each child.

Have the children choose something from their poems and draw a large picture of it on their grid papers. Ask them to write or print their names in the rectangles either inside or outside their drawings. Their names act like paints to color areas and highlight their pictures.

Signature of a frog
jumps from lily pad to lily pad.

Signature of a cheetah
runs through the savanna.

Signature of a snake
slithers through the grass.

Noah Baker, age 5

SIGNATURES

The signature of a lion
is on the ground.
The signature of a crow
is in the sky.
The signature of a frog is hopping.
The signature of a fish
swims in the bowl.

Rachel Podell-Eberhardt, age 5

Signature of a rock
is hard and lumpy.
Signature of a turtle
is smooth and wet.

Tosten Haugerud, age 7

Signature of the lion
roars like the sun setting.
The handwriting of the parrot
looks like a rainbow
setting over a cloud.

Lucas Powers, age 7

WRITING

The signature of a cougar
rolls down a mountain.
The handwriting of a horse
gallops in the meadow.
The handwriting of a banana
is stuck in its peel.

Montana Tippett, age 8

From *Word Weavings: Writing Poetry with Young Children* published by Good Year Books. Copyright © 1997 Shelley Tucker.

Open a Poem

Description

Start with a key and watch it open a door to creativity.

In this exercise, children begin lines in their poems with the words *open* and *start*. These words work like keys to open colors and feelings or start rainbows and spring. The children begin the last lines of their poems with the phrase "It is the key of." Then they use keys or templates of keys to illustrate their poetry.

Presentation

Write the following words on the board and review them with the children:

open	start

Tell them that in poetry, we might write about opening a door to a house or starting a car. Poetry also enables us to suggest more unusual activities. For example, we could write "open love" or "start July."

Ask the children to begin with the word *open* and then name a place outside.

Examples:
> Open the forest.
> Open a park.
> Open the playground.

Then ask them to start with the word *open* and name a time of day.

Examples:
> Open morning.
> Open 11:00 A.M.

After a few responses, ask some of the following questions to show the children how to extend their ideas:

> *What's inside it? What happens then? What will you see?*

Example:
> **CHILD:** *Open morning.*
>
> **TEACHER:** *What happens then?*
>
> **SAME OR ANOTHER CHILD:** *You eat cereal.*
>
> **TEACHER:** *We can put the two parts together and say, "Open morning. You eat cereal."*

Art Materials

- Construction paper in two or more colors
- Pencils, crayons, or markers
- Scissors
- Tape or staplers
- Actual keys or template of keys

Then ask the children to begin with the word *start* and add the name of a season.

Examples:	*Start autumn.*
	Start summer.

After a few responses, ask some of the following questions to help the children extend their ideas:

What happens then? What does it do? Where does it go? Why?

Example:

CHILD: *Start autumn.*

TEACHER: *Why?*

SAME OR ANOTHER CHILD: *So we can watch the leaves fall.*

TEACHER: *Who can put the two parts together?*

CHILD OR TEACHER: *Start autumn so we can watch the leaves fall.*

(After some practice, the children will learn to combine the parts of the sentences independently.)

Then tell the children that they will begin the last line of their poems with the phrase "It is the key of." The word *key* here means an important part of something. For example, we could say "Open morning. You eat cereal. It is the key of a good day."

Example:

TEACHER: *Who will start with the phrase "It is the key of," and name something important about autumn?*

CHILD: *It is the key of color.*

TEACHER: *Here's our whole poem:*

> *Start autumn*
> *so we can watch the leaves fall.*
> *It is the key of color.*

From *Word Weavings: Writing Poetry with Young Children* published by Good Year Books. Copyright © 1997 Shelley Tucker.

Practice

Provide the children with more practice by doing this exercise.

■ Write the following categories on the board:

> places outside
> times of day
> seasons
> weather
> fruits or vegetables
> holidays
> colors
> feelings
> sports
> things in the sky

■ Select a category. Ask the children to begin with either *open* or *start,* and then add an example from the category.

■ Ask the questions to show them how to extend their ideas. *Optional: Have them compose a second sentence on the same topic.*

■ Now ask the children to start the last lines of their poems with the phrase "It is the key of." Suggest they add a word they haven't already used in their poems.

Writing Poetry

Tell the children to begin their poems with *open* or *start* and begin the last lines of their poems with the words "It is the key of."

Making Art

Give each child a template of a key or an actual key. Locksmiths often provide old keys for teachers to use in their classrooms. Ask the children to illustrate their poems using the keys in their art.

For variation, give each child two pieces of construction paper in different colors. Have them draw windows and doors on one piece of paper and cut out three sides of each shape so they open. Next, ask them to staple the sheet of paper with the doors and windows on top of the other piece. The children can draw pictures behind their doors and windows.

Start eating your fruits and vegetables

like apples, carrots, oranges,

bananas, blackberries,

corn, and grapes.

They are the key

of the food pyramid,

strength, growth,

and less fat.

Alex Korbonits, age 8

Open the door of the jungle.

It is the key of the tiger.

Open the door of the eagle world.

It is the key of sight.

Sean Fithian, age 7

PICKLE

Open a pickle and find treasures,

gems, precious stones,

and some pickle juice.

It is the key of a stomachache.

Amelia Gallaher, age 7

Start a sunny day

with flowers in the ground.

Flowers grow in the backyard.

They are the key to my mom.

Hanah Lee Ho, age 6

Open the sun

when it's a rainy day.

It is the key of a rainbow.

Allegra Condiotty, age 5

Personification

Personification means assigning human traits to animals and things.

VOICE OF NIGHT

I think I heard

the voice of the sunset

in the evening sky

when all the people

were eating dinner.

Heart of a rug

with a kitten circled up

by the fire,

so soft and so gentle,

made the rug's heart brighten.

The voice of the moon

talked to the coyote,

so dark and so quiet,

in the night.

Olivia Hoffmeyer, age 7

Children can try out personification using just a few words. Consider the following examples:

Waves whisper.
Trees dance.
A computer sighs.

The assignment of any human trait to animals or things creates personification. In "There's an Octopus in My Kitchen," animals live in houses and apartments doing human activities. In the exercise "Voice of the Heart," the children endow objects with human characteristics: a voice, the hands, and a heart. The model "Conversations of Cows" shows children how to write poems about objects and animals that talk. In "Alligators Brush Their Teeth," animals perform human actions in a variety of places. In "Stars Dance at Night," children assign human activities to parts of the natural environment.

Personification works like a great actor in a play. She walks onto the stage of the page and recites her lines with flair. We listen, and personification tells us poetry.

From *Word Weavings: Writing Poetry with Young Children* published by Good Year Books. Copyright © 1997 Shelley Tucker.

There's an Octopus in My Kitchen

Art Materials

- Construction or drawing paper

- Glue

- Tagboard frames, or strips of tagboard or construction paper to make frames

- Tissue paper, canceled stamps, pictures from magazines, shells, or other things to decorate the frames

Description

Imagine an animal in a house or apartment doing a common human activity. Perhaps an octopus washes dishes in the kitchen or a kangaroo writes poetry in the living room.

In this exercise, the children compose interesting and unusual poems by describing animals doing ordinary human activities in the rooms of apartments or houses. Then they draw the animals and frame the pictures to represent the rooms.

Presentation

Ask the children to name animals. Tell them they are going to imagine animals in rooms of their houses or apartments doing things people usually do. Then ask them the following questions:

- ■ "What is the animal?"
- ■ "What room is it in?"
- ■ "What is it doing?" (Ask them to name something a person does.)

Example:

> **TEACHER:** *What animal is in your apartment or house?*
>
> **CHILD:** *An elephant.*
>
> **TEACHER:** *What room is it in?*
>
> **SAME OR ANOTHER CHILD:** *The living room.*
>
> **TEACHER:** *What is it doing? Name something a person usually does.*
>
> **SAME OR ANOTHER CHILD:** *It is watching TV and operating the remote control with its trunk.*

Provide the children with practice answering the three questions and work with them on forming complete sentences.

From *Word Weavings: Writing Poetry with Young Children* published by Good Year Books. Copyright © 1997 Shelley Tucker.

Example:

> **TEACHER:** *What animal is in your apartment or house?*
>
> **CHILD:** *A dog.*
>
> **TEACHER:** *What room is it in?*
>
> **SAME OR ANOTHER CHILD:** *The basement.*
>
> **TEACHER:** *What is it doing? Name something a person usually does.*
>
> **SAME OR ANOTHER CHILD:** *Lifting weights.*
>
> **TEACHER:** *Who will say the first sentence for a poem about a dog lifting weights?*
>
> **FIRST CHILD:** *There's a dog in my basement lifting weights.*
>
> **TEACHER:** *How else could we start this poem?*
>
> **SECOND CHILD:** *I have a dog. He's in my basement lifting weights.*

Practice

Give the children practice by doing this exercise:

- Ask the questions: What is the animal? What room is it in? What is it doing? (Ask them to name something a person does.)
- Have them form complete sentences.

Writing Poetry

Tell the children to write or say poems about animals doing ordinary human activities in rooms of houses or apartments. Children might write about one or many animals.

Making Art

Ask the children to draw pictures of the animals in their poems behaving like humans. Have them decorate tagboard frames, strips of tagboard, or construction paper with squares of tissue paper, canceled stamps, soup labels, gum wrappers, stickers, or small pictures and place the frames around their drawings to represent rooms.

LOOK WHAT'S IN MY HOUSE

Yesterday I saw a kangaroo

doing the laundry.

Today I heard a hippopotamus

in my bathroom brushing his teeth.

Michael Diaz, age 7

In my dad's office,

a shark is playing the computer.

In my bathroom

an elephant is taking a shower.

Will Scott, age 7

In my kitchen there is an octopus

eating waffles

with butter and syrup.

In my living room there is a fish

eating some meatballs.

Harry Howell, age 5

MY HOUSE

In my living room

there is a lizard watching TV.

In my bedroom,

there is a shark drawing.

In my backyard,

there is an emerald tree snake

slithering through the trees.

Noam Nicholson, age 5

There are creatures in my computer room.

There are lions licking lollipops

in my living room.

There is a baboon being bad

in my dining room.

He's wearing my clothes

and they don't fit.

Scott Morse, age 8

From *Word Weavings: Writing Poetry with Young Children* published by Good Year Books. Copyright © 1997 Shelley Tucker.

Voice of the Earth

Description

In the heart of a poem dwells a voice. It tells of a turtle on a riverbed, speaks of a salmon swimming upstream, and sings about the journey of the wind.

In this exercise, children use the phrases "voice of," "heart of" and "hands of" to describe things, feelings, and colors. Then they make heart baskets to hold or illustrate their poems.

Presentation

Write the following words on the board and review them with the children:

> *voice of*
> *heart of*
> *hands of*

Tell them that poems, we might write about the voices, hands, and hearts of people. Poetry also gives us a way to explore the voice of a refrigerator, the heart of the winter, or the hands of a tree.

Have the children start with the phrase "voice of" and add the name of some type of weather.

Examples:
> *voice of the tornado*
> *voice of snow*

After a few responses, ask some of the following questions to show them how to extend their ideas:

> *Does what? Says what? Is where?*
> *Sounds like what? Tells you what?*

Example:
> **CHILD:** *Voice of a storm.*
> **TEACHER:** *Does what?*
> **SAME OR ANOTHER CHILD:** *Talks to me.*
> **TEACHER:** *We can put both parts together and say, "Voice of the storm talks to me."*

Have the children start with the phrase "heart of" and name something that grows outside.

From *Word Weavings: Writing Poetry with Young Children* published by Good Year Books. Copyright © 1997 Shelley Tucker.

- Sheets of paper, 8-1/2 by 8-1/2 inches (21.59 by 21.59 cm), one per child

- Ribbon or yarn, 8 inches (20.32 cm) long, 1 per child

- Tape or stapler

From *Word Weavings: Writing Poetry with Young Children* published by Good Year Books. Copyright © 1997 Shelley Tucker.

Examples:

> heart of an apple
> heart of a tree

After a few responses, ask some of the following questions to show them how to extend their ideas:

> *Feels what? Knows what? Wants what? Remembers what?*
> *Is where? Tells us what? Looks like what?*

Example:

> **CHILD:** *Heart of an apple.*
> **TEACHER:** *Looks like what?*
> **SAME OR ANOTHER CHILD:** *A star.*
> **TEACHER:** *Who can put the two parts together?*
> **CHILD OR ADULT:** *Heart of an apple looks like a star.*

Next, have the children start with the phrase "hands of" and add the name of a machine.

Examples:

> hands of the car
> hands of an airplane

After some responses, ask these questions:

> *Do what? Want what? Are where? Look like what? Reach for what?*

Example:

> **CHILD:** *Hands of a car.*
> **TEACHER:** *Do what?*
> **SAME OR ANOTHER CHILD:** *Pump gas.*
> **TEACHER:** *Who can put the two parts together?*
> **SAME OR ANOTHER CHILD:** *Hands of a car pump gas.*

Practice

Repeat these steps a number of times to give the children more practice:

■ Write these categories on the board and choose one:

> | | | |
> |---|---|---|
> | colors | things in the ocean | objects in the sky |
> | holidays | objects in a house | months |

■ Have the children begin with the phrases "voice of," "heart of," or "hands of," and add an example from the category.

■ Then ask questions to show children how to extend their ideas.

Writing Poetry

Tell the children to write poems about objects, colors, and feelings using the phrases "voice of," "heart of," and "hands of." Remind them of the categories of things they might name. For variation, ask the children for other ways to start their poems or suggest:

> *Have you ever heard the voice of*
> *Have you ever seen the hands of*
> *Have you ever felt/known the heart of*
> *I heard the voice of*
> *I saw the hands of*
> *I felt/knew the heart of*

Making Art

The children make folded hearts to use as baskets that illustrate or store their poems.

First, have the children fold a sheet of 8-1/2 by 8-1/2-inch (21.59 by 21.59 cm) paper in half, and then fold it in half again to form a square. Next, they turn the square so it looks like a diamond with the two folded edges pointing down. Ask them to fold the right side of the diamond over to the left and crease it to make a triangle. Next, have them rotate the top of the shape slightly to the right, so it looks like an ice cream cone. They then cut off the top of the shape with a circular cut to form a rounded top that looks like a scoop of ice cream.

Tell the children to open their sheets of paper. Some of the folds in the paper will face up while other folds face down. Finding the two folds opposite each other that face up, they should push these two folds together and hold them with one hand. Two heart-shaped pockets will form. Have the children push these pockets together to flatten them. The final, folded piece of paper has a heart shape on each side with two folds touching on the inside. Ask the children to punch holes at the top of the heart and insert ribbon to form a handle. Each child can make one or many hearts to illustrate or hold their poetry.

RAINBOW

The voice of a rainbow

is taking a nap.

The hands of a rainbow

are playing loudly in peace.

Chelsea Maddock, age 5

HEART

Heart of the door

opens into another new world—

hands of the garden,

rings of roses,

lavender scents of herbs,

and a garland of flowers.

Anna Crandall, age 8

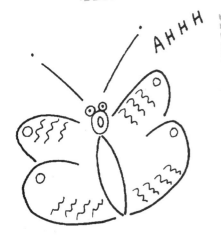

AHHH

LOVE

The voice of love

fills the sky with freedom.

The heart of the land

is covered with love.

The feet of love

are like butterfly sneezes.

Anne Riepe, age 9

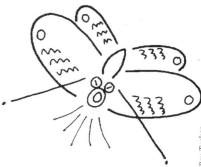

CHOO!

SKY

The voice of the sky

tells me it's hot outside.

I want to go out and play, but I can't.

The hands of the sun are too hot.

Soon, though, the bodies of the clouds

will block out the sun,

so I can play. I hope.

Walter Thorn, age 8

The hands of the gate

reach for the metal.

The voice of the ocean,

quiet and pretty,

whistles in the trees.

Harry Howell, age 5

From *Word Weavings: Writing Poetry with Young Children* published by Good Year Books. Copyright © 1997 Shelley Tucker.

Conversations of Cows

Description

If the wind talked, what would it sound like? If cows had a conversation, what would they say?

In this exercise, children use the phrases "words of," "conversations of," and "language of" to describe things. Then they make three-dimensional figures that stand in groups as though engaged in conversation.

Presentation

Write the following words on the board and review them with the children:

> *words of*
> *conversations of*
> *language of*

Tell the children that we often hear what people say and the conversations they have. We can use poetry to describe more unusual interactions. For example, we might write about the words of a watermelon or the conversations of clouds.

Ask the children to start with the phrase "words of" and name an animal.

Examples: | *words of alligators*
words of chipmunks

After a few responses, ask some of the following questions to show them how to extend their ideas:

> *Talk about what? Remember what? Sound like what? Do what?*

Example: | **CHILD:** *Words of an alligator.*

TEACHER: *Sound like what?*

SAME OR ANOTHER CHILD: *Drums.*

TEACHER: *We can put both parts together and say, "Words of an alligator sound like drums."*

From *Word Weavings: Writing Poetry with Young Children* published by Good Year Books. Copyright © 1997 Shelley Tucker.

Art Materials

- Tagboard or construction paper, 6 by 9 inches (15.24 by 22.86 cm), a few pieces per child

- Pencil, crayons, or marker

- Scissors

- Glue or tape

Then ask the children to start with the phrase "words of" and add the name of a color.

Examples:	*words of green*
	words of red

After a few responses, ask questions to show them how to extend their ideas:

> *Talk about what? Remember what? Sound like what? Do what?*

Example:

> **CHILD:** *Words of green.*
>
> **TEACHER:** *Do what?*
>
> **SAME OR ANOTHER CHILD:** *Whisper at night.*
>
> **CHILD OR TEACHER:** *We can put both parts together and say, "Words of green whisper at night."*

Practice

Give the children more practice using the phrase "words of."

■ Write these categories on the board and choose one:

> *transportation*
> *sports*
> *times of day*
> *things that grow in parks*
> *musical instruments*
> *weather*
> *things in the sky*
> *food*

■ Have the children start with the phrase "words of," and add examples from that category.

■ After each response, ask some of the following questions to help them extend their ideas:

> *Talk about what? Remember what? Sound like what? Do what?*

(With practice, the children will learn to easily combine the parts of the sentences themselves.)

■ Repeat the steps using the phrase "conversation of."
  Optional: Use the phrase "language of."

Writing Poetry

Tell the children to write or say poems describing interactions with the phrases "words of," "conversation of," and "language of." Review the list of categories. For variation, ask them for other ways they might start their poems or suggest:

> *Have you heard the words, conversations, language of*
> *I heard (or listened to) the words, conversations, language of*

Making Art

For this art project, the children fold pieces of tagboard in half to create figures that stand.

To make animals, the folds in the board become the tops of their backs. First, have the children draw the bodies and legs of animals on the tagboard. Then they cut out the animals, leaving the folds intact to create two symmetrical connected shapes. Next, ask them to draw, cut out, and attach the heads and tails.

The children can make other figures, such as trees, cars, and stars, with the folds at the tops of the shapes. When they cut out their drawings, they leave some part of the folds intact to form identical connected shapes that stand. Have them arrange these figures in groups, so that an alligator, owl, and ant or perhaps the wind, sun, and moon seem engaged in conversation.

I listened to the giraffes

having a conversation

with the monkeys.

I listened to the words of the spider.

I listened to the wind

talking to the trees.

Casey Ikeda, age 6

CONVERSATION

Have you ever heard

clams have a conversation?

Clip Clop,

Clip Clop.

Have you ever heard

the scrambled eggs

talking to each other saying,

Ouch, Ouch,

this pan's too hot?

Katelyn Melvey, age 7

WILLOW WHISPERING

Have you ever heard a willow

whispering over a clear blue lake?

Have you ever heard

the conversation

of the violins and cellos,

so beautiful and soft?

Anna Crandall, age 8

I listen to the words of the trees

singing quietly.

The wind of the flowers

curls up into little balls

and falls slowly.

Chelsea Maddock, age 6

Thoughts of the rainbow bring color.

The conversation of the world gives light.

Language of the sun gives me life.

The words of the sea listen to me.

Samuel Heller, age 8

From *Word Weavings: Writing Poetry with Young Children* published by Good Year Books. Copyright © 1997 Shelley Tucker.

Alligators Brush Their Teeth

Description

Imagine a cat using a computer, a bear cooking breakfast, or a frog playing basketball. Writing poetry gives children a way to do just that.

In this exercise, children write about animals doing human activities. Then they make animal masks with three-dimensional noses.

Presentation

Tell children that we might write poems about things animals usually do. We could describe, for example, a cat climbing a tree or a dog chasing a stick. Poetry also gives us a way to write about more unusual events, such as an ant jumping rope or a rhinoceros riding a bike.

Ask the children to name a variety of animals.

Then write the following categories of things people do horizontally across the board:

Things people do:	*at school*
	at work
	for fun
	at recess
	on the weekends
	in sports
	at night

Ask the children to give many examples of each and then list their responses under the categories.

Now show them how to form sentences, pairing the animals with the human actions.

Example:	**TEACHER:** *Who will name an animal?*
	CHILD: *Dog.*
	TEACHER: *Who will name something people do at school?*
	SAME OR ANOTHER CHILD: *Study.*
	TEACHER: *We can put these together and say, "A dog studies."*

From *Word Weavings: Writing Poetry with Young Children* published by Good Year Books. Copyright © 1997 Shelley Tucker.

Next, ask some of the following questions to show the children how to extend their ideas:

> *Where? When? Why? How? What time of day?*

Example:

> **TEACHER:** *Who will name an animal?*
>
> **CHILD:** *Cat.*
>
> **TEACHER:** *Who will name something people do on Saturday?*
>
> **SAME OR ANOTHER CHILD:** *Mow the lawn.*
>
> **TEACHER:** *Who will put both parts together?*
>
> **TEACHER OR CHILD:** *A cat mows the lawn.*
>
> **TEACHER:** *What time of day?*
>
> **SAME OR ANOTHER CHILD:** *In the morning.*
>
> **TEACHER:** *Who will put it all together?*
>
> **TEACHER OR CHILD:** *A cat mows the lawn in the morning.*

(After some practice, the children will learn to combine the phrases by themselves.)

Practice

Provide more practice by doing this exercise:

- Ask the children to name an animal.
- Have them add the name of something a person does.
- Ask some questions to show them how to extend their ideas.

Writing Poetry

Tell the children to write or say poems about animals doing the things people usually do. Then ask them to lengthen their sentences. Review the list of categories to remind them of the many types of human activities they might name. For variety, ask the children for other ways they might start their poems.

From *Word Weavings: Writing Poetry with Young Children* published by Good Year Books. Copyright © 1997 Shelley Tucker.

Making Art

Have the children make masks with three-dimensional noses to illustrate the animals in their poems. Give the children paper plates. Ask them to measure and draw the eyes and mouth, and cut them out.

Next the children can make the noses. First, provide them with 3-inch (7.62 cm) square papers to fold in half. Have them cut a line, 1-1/2 inches (3.81 cm) long, perpendicular to the fold. (For noses with different shapes, have the children make curved rather than straight cuts.) Then they fold the flap backwards and pinch the crease together. Next, they push the folded triangle through to the other side of the paper to create the three-dimensional nose.

Have the children glue the noses onto the paper plates and poke breathing holes under them. Now they can decorate their masks. To use the masks, the children cut a slit above ear level in both sides of their plates and punch a hole above the slits for the string. They might also use a craft stick taped to the bottom of each plate to hold it.

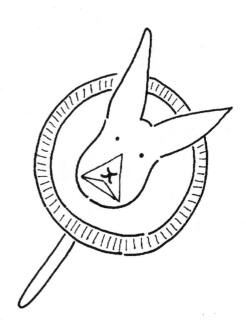

I was in my house watching TV,

and I saw a cheetah playing video games.

The cheetah saw a kangaroo playing hopscotch.

The kangaroo saw a person watching TV,

and that person was me.

Casey Ikeda, age 6

RECESS

Seals play hopscotch.

Bunnies jump on pogo sticks.

Monkeys bounce on trampolines.

Noam Nicholson, age 6

Raccoons fix shingles on the roof.

Kangaroos jump rope.

Bats hang on a trapeze.

Possums ride bikes on the handle bars

turning upside down.

Evan Bang, age 6

DRAGON

A dragon roasts marshmallows

in the forest.

There are lots of trees around him.

He uses his mouth to blow fire

on the marshmallows

and he makes them golden brown.

Dane Hendricksen, age 5

From *Word Weavings: Writing Poetry with Young Children* published by Good Year Books. Copyright © 1997 Shelley Tucker.

Stars Dance at Night

Description

Imagine a leaf laughing, the ocean waving, or the moon winking.

In this exercise, the children describe natural elements performing human actions. Then they make three-dimensional cards to illustrate their scenes.

Presentation

Tell the children that, in poetry, we might write about a girl singing or a boy laughing. Poetry also allows us to assign human behaviors to things. We could say, for example, that a breeze sings or the moon laughs.

List on the board the following categories of things in nature and ask the children to suggest examples of them. Write their responses under each category.

> *weather*
> *seasons*
> *things in the sky*
> *objects that grow in forests*
> *things in the ocean*
> *types of bodies of water*
> *minerals and metals*

Then have the children name things people do:

> *on holidays*
> *after school*
> *on Saturdays*
> *in sports*
> *at home*

List their responses on the board. They do not need to be grouped by their category.

Examples:
> *wash clothes*
> *sleep*
> *talk on the phone*
> *mow the lawn*
> *feed the cat*
> *sing*

From *Word Weavings: Writing Poetry with Young Children* published by Good Year Books. Copyright © 1997 Shelley Tucker.

Art Materials

- Construction paper, 9 by 12 inches, in different colors, 2 pieces per child
- Pencils, crayons, or markers
- Scissors
- Glue

Then ask the children to choose something in nature and add a human action. They may use the words on the board or suggest other ones.

Example:

> **TEACHER:** *Who will name a type of weather?*
>
> **CHILD:** *Rain.*
>
> **TEACHER:** *Who will name something a person does?*
>
> **SAME OR ANOTHER CHILD:** *Talks.*
>
> **TEACHER:** *We can put these together and say, "Rain talks."*

Review this part of the exercise with children until they can independently pair the human behaviors with the elements of nature. Practice this by pointing to the respective lists on the board. Then ask the following questions to show the children how to extend their ideas.

> *Where? When? Why? How?*

Example:

> **TEACHER:** *Who will name something that grows in the forest and then have it perform a human action?*
>
> **CHILD:** *A tree plays chess.*
>
> **TEACHER:** *How does a tree play chess?*
>
> **SAME OR ANOTHER CHILD:** *With its roots.*
>
> **TEACHER:** *We can put both parts together and say, "A tree plays chess with its roots."*

(With practice, children will learn to combine the phrases by themselves.)

Practice

Provide them with more practice by doing this exercise:

- Have the children name something in nature and then add a human action. They may use the words on the board or suggest different ones.

- Ask some questions to show them ways to extend their ideas.

From *Word Weavings: Writing Poetry with Young Children* published by Good Year Books. Copyright © 1997 Shelley Tucker.

Writing Poetry

Tell the children to will write or say poems giving objects in nature human behaviors. Review the words on the board to show them some of the many things they might name.

Making Art

The children make cards with scenes that pop out when opened.

First, ask the children to fold a piece of construction paper in half to form the outside of the card. Now have them fold a second piece of paper in half and then in half again, so it is long and thin. As they open it on their desks and point the center fold up, all of the folds will be in an accordion pattern except for one. Have them refold that crease so the paper is pleated like an accordion.

Now tell the children to place the pleated paper on their desks, center fold up, and illustrate their poems on it. When they finish their drawings, they can cut out the tops and bottoms of their pictures to form silhouettes. Have them glue the end panels of the pleated sheet onto the outer card with the center fold of the outside card facing down, and the center crease of the inside sheet pointing up. When the children open their cards, silhouettes of mountains, trees, and stars will pop out and greet them.

THE PEACEFUL JUNGLE

In the jungle the flower waves.

The river runs to call to you.

The lion purrs softly.

A toucan calls to say good-bye to you.

From a far away tree,

a parrot says, I will see you soon,

and that parrot is me.

Katelyn Melvey, age 7

The river tiptoes on rocks

while the moon

sings songs for the stars.

Karol Neavor, age 8

MOTHER EARTH

Did you know

Mother Earth's eyes walk?

They're animals.

We eat the earth's dreams.

They're fish.

When I'm in a tree,

I'm sitting in Mother Earth's hair.

Caitlin Wilson, age 6

see you soon!

THE MOUNTAIN AND THE TREE

The mountain tells the tree

to put on his green hat.

The mountain looks at tree and thinks,

"Tree, you're still missing your coat."

Duyen My Nguyen, age 8

Water cries

goodbye, goodbye

as it flows down the river.

Kirsten Day, age 5

From *Word Weavings: Writing Poetry with Young Children* published by Good Year Books. Copyright © 1997 Shelley Tucker.

Alliteration

Alliteration repeats initial consonant sounds in words close together.

Jets of jaguars

jet to the race.

Skis of snakes

go to school.

Roller blades of dinosaurs

skate to their desks.

Sleds of spiders

dance at the ball.

Ben Lukes, age 7

Using alliteration creates a letter orchestra. Ts tap, Rs roll, Ss slide, Bs brush, and Ds drum into a symphony of words on paper. Consider the following examples of alliteration:

Loving lions pick lilacs and give them to other animals.

Turtles try to turn quickly but see they'll get there sooner if they go slowly.

Yesterday, I saw a bus bulging with balloons that bounced against the windows.

Alliteration is like rhyme at the beginnings of words rather than at the ends. In the exercise "Cars of Kangaroos," the children write alliteration with nouns, naming vehicles and the things in them. In "Penguins Like to Paint," they create alliteration between nouns and verbs.

Remember tongue twisters? They're examples of alliteration using interesting subjects and sounds.

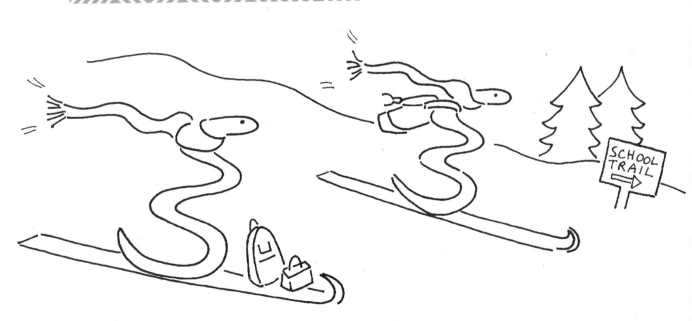

SCHOOL TRAIL

Cars of Kangaroos

From *Word Weavings: Writing Poetry with Young Children* published by Good Year Books. Copyright © 1997 Shelley Tucker.

Art Materials

- Construction paper

- Pencils, crayons, or markers

- Tape or glue

- Scissors

- Milk containers, egg cartons, plastic bottles, margarine tubs

- Bottle tops, paper towel tubes

Description

Sound poems engage the ears and eyes. Consider the sentence "Slugs ride on sleds." The sound of s enhances the image of the slugs on sleds slushing and sliding through snow.

In this exercise, the children name vehicles and write about things in them that start with the same sounds. Next, they make small models of their vehicles from food containers.

Presentation

Ask the children to name several forms of transportation. To stimulate their thinking, suggest places where vehicles usually travel, such as in the sky, on the water, and on the ground. Then write the names of the vehicles in a list on the board. They do not need to be grouped by the category.

Examples:

car
jet
plane
boat
ship
submarine
canoe
truck
ferry

Tell the children that in poetry, we might write about a car of people or a truck of groceries. Poems also give us a way to describe imaginative situations, for example, a boat of bologna or a canoe carrying cats.

Choose one of the vehicles listed on the board and have the children name things in it that start with the same sound.

Example:

> **TEACHER:** *Let's pretend that we have a jet filled with things that begin with the sound* j. *We could say we have a jet of jewels. What else starts with* j *that could be in this jet?*
>
> **FIRST CHILD:** *Jelly.*
>
> **SECOND CHILD:** *Jam.*
>
> **THIRD CHILD:** *Juice.*
>
> **FOURTH CHILD:** *Jaguars.*

Then work with the children on forming complete sentences. Suggest the following line starts if needed:

> *Have you ever seen*
> *I saw*
> *There is a*

Example with all the steps:

> **TEACHER:** *Who will begin with one of these (pointing to the line starts on the board) and then name a type of vehicle?*
>
> **CHILD:** *Have you ever seen a bus?*
>
> **TEACHER:** *Now let's pretend that this bus has things in it that start with the sound* b. *These can be objects that do or don't really fit in it. Who will say a sentence that begins, "Have you ever seen a bus with," and then name things that start with the sound* b?
>
> **SAME OR ANOTHER CHILD:** *Have you ever seen a bus with bears and baboons?*
>
> **ANOTHER CHILD:** *Have you ever seen a bus with baseballs, basketballs, and baseball players?*

Practice

Give the children practice by doing this exercise:

- Choose a type of transportation.

- Have the children compose sentences about what's in or on it. Suggest line starts if needed. Remind them to name vehicles and then contents that start with the same sound.

- Ask questions to show them ways to extend their sentences.

Writing Poetry

Tell the children to write or say poems about different kinds of vehicles. Review the steps in this exercise with them.

Making Art

Containers commonly found in kitchens provide excellent materials for models of vehicles. Egg cartons, margarine tubs, and water bottles have a lot in common with cars, planes, and vans. These containers keep their contents safe for travel from one place to another.

Give the children plastic bottles, egg cartons, milk containers, and cereal boxes to make the frames of their vehicles. Bottle tops and paper towel rolls make great wheels. Have the children fill their vehicles with drawings of objects from their poems.

There was a car with 2,000 cats in it
and a bus that only had bees.
I saw a pegasus with a person
on his back and a bus with bears
with bows on their heads.

Ariel Cartwright, age 6

I saw a wagon carrying water
and a boat full of big buffaloes.
I saw a camel carrying a car
with crates of canned caterpillars
and caramels and a truck
carrying tanks of tickle potion.

Olivia Hoffmeyer, age 7

HAVE YOU EVER SEEN?

Have you ever seen a boat
carrying a cart of bananas,
bows, and belt buckles?
I saw a subway with a silly singer
and a ferryboat with funny clowns.
I also saw a train with turtles.

Alison Haruta, age 6

SLEDS

Sleds of sausages,
sauerkraut, sugar,
shrimp, and soda
slide slowly in the snow.

Robert Suarez, age 8

CARS

Cars of kids can't sit still.
They talk and talk
and talk and talk.
Cars of kangaroos
hop to school
and jump across the traffic.
Cars of cats
always chase dogs,
meow, woof, meow, woof.

Michael Dela Cruz, age 8

Penguins Like to Paint

Art Materials

- Paper plates

- Pencils, crayons, or markers

- Scissors

- Tape

Description

Alliteration is often funny.

In this exercise, the children name animals and actions that start with the same sounds. Then they make paper plate animals to illustrate their poems.

Presentation

Ask the children to name a variety of animals. Then have them choose one and add a word to it that begins with the same sound.

Examples:

> *Bears brush.*
> *Dogs drive.*
> *Lions laugh.*

After a few examples, ask some of the following questions to show them how to extend their ideas:

> *Where? When? Why? How?*

Example:

> **CHILD:** *Bears brush.*
>
> **TEACHER:** *What?*
>
> **SAME OR ANOTHER CHILD:** *Their fur.*
>
> **TEACHER:** *We can put both parts together and say, "Bears brush their fur."*

Example with all the steps:

> **TEACHER:** *Who will name an animal?*
>
> **CHILD:** *Zebra.*
>
> **TEACHER:** *Who will add an action word that starts with the sound z?*
>
> **SAME OR ANOTHER CHILD:** *Zoom.*
>
> **TEACHER:** *Who will put both words together?*
>
> **SAME OR ANOTHER CHILD:** *Zebras zoom.*
>
> **TEACHER:** *Now who will start with the phrase "zebras zoom," and say where they zoom?*
>
> **SAME OR ANOTHER CHILD:** *Zebras zoom to the zoo.*

(After practice, children will combine the phrases by themselves.)

From *Word Weavings: Writing Poetry with Young Children* published by Good Year Books. Copyright © 1997 Shelley Tucker.

Practice

Provide them with more practice by doing this exercise:

- Ask the children to name an animal.

- Have them add an action word that starts with the same sound.

- Then ask some of the following questions to show them how to extend their ideas:

> *Where? When? Why? How?*

Writing Poetry

Review all the steps with the children, including ways to extend their ideas.

Making Art

Here are some of the many animals the children can make from paper plates:

Turtle: Fold a paper plate in half, point the round part up for the turtle's shell, and the attach the head, feet, and tail.

Lion: Fringe the outside of the plate for a lion's head.

Swan: Cut off the outside rim of the plate, and use it as the neck and head. Then make the body following directions for the turtle.

Snake: Cut a paper plate in a spiral to create a snake.

Owl: Make cuts in the plate at two, four, eight, and ten o'clock positions. Then fold the sides in toward the center for feathers.

Children can design animals in a variety of ways using paper plates shaped with the scissors of their imaginations.

SLITHERS

A snake slithers

through the stars

and the moon

in the Milky Way.

Nicholas Boroughs, age 7

BEAVERS AND BIRDS

A beaver builds a house

curved as a piece of wood,

round as the top of a pencil.

A bird constructs a nest

round as a candy cane.

Osani Shapiro, age 5

DINOSAURS DON'T USE MANNERS

Bobcats burn bacon on the stove.

Snakes snatch spaghetti.

Dinosaurs don't use manners.

Graham Stockdale, age 8

THE SNAKE

The snake slips slowly

through the grass.

Aaron Graham, age 7

Cats cannot handle leashes.

Dogs dream about bones.

Snakes seem shy but they're not.

Turtles take a long time to walk.

Alex Johnston, age 8

From *Word Weavings: Writing Poetry with Young Children* published by Good Year Books. Copyright © 1997 Shelley Tucker.

Onomatopoeia

Onomatopoeia uses words that imitate or suggest the sounds they describe.

Children love onomatopoeia. Consider some of these obvious examples of it:

meow, crash, crack, slurp, twirl, screech, bow wow

Some onomatopoeic words can be more subtle. Say the word *wail,* and your mouth opens wide. Pronounce the word *bite,* and you do the action, too. Notice how your lips arch when you say the word *round.*

Have fun with onomatopoeia. One note of caution, however. Writing poetry with onomatopoeia can get noisy. Children do not just speak these words. They often make accompanying sound effects too. Give them a little time to act out the sounds, and then they will focus on the words used to make them.

MY MACHINE

My machine studies animals

at the museum.

It feeds the dog food and water.

My machine goes,

swoosh, plop, and scoop.

It writes about animals

and sounds like scribble.

Sara Vichorek, age 5

Whoosh!

From *Word Weavings: Writing Poetry with Young Children* published by Good Year Books. Copyright © 1997 Shelley Tucker.

Art Materials

- Tagboard or construction paper

- Pencils, crayons, or markers

- String

- Things to create sounds, such as hardware, clothes pins, popsicle sticks, twigs, stones, paper clips

Description

Children know the sounds of things. Ask them to describe the sound of the wind, and they can easily recall the way it rustles and hisses the leaves as it moves through the trees. Talk with them about a train, and they know the sound "choo choo" is as much a part of it as the wheels and tracks.

In this exercise, the children list activities, things, and places that generate lots of sounds. Then they name the sounds and use these and others in their poems. Next, the children design soundmakers by hanging things close together that chime, clang, or ring when they move.

Presentation

Ask the children to name things, places, and activities that make many sounds.

Examples:

> birds
> airplanes
> radios
> oceans
> sports stadiums
> schools
> bowling
> washing dishes
> cooking

List their suggestions horizontally across the top of the board. Then ask the children to name the sounds these things make and list these under the headings.

Examples:

> **AIRPLANES:** *roar, rumble, screech*
> **BOWLING:** *roll, splat, groan*
> **WASHING DISHES:** *swish, click, swirl, squeak*

Choose one of the topics from the board. Have them compose sentences about it.

From *Word Weavings: Writing Poetry with Young Children* published by Good Year Books. Copyright © 1997 Shelley Tucker.

Example:

> **TEACHER:** *Who will suggest the first line of a poem about bowling?*
>
> **CHILD:** *I like to go bowling on Saturdays.*
>
> **TEACHER:** *Who will say another sentence about bowling?*
>
> **SAME OR ANOTHER CHILD:** *My mom takes me to the lanes.*

Then ask the children to include related sounds.

Example:

> **TEACHER:** *What sounds do we hear in bowling?*
>
> **CHILD:** *Roll, bam, cheer, crash.*
>
> **TEACHER:** *How can we use those sounds in a sentence?*
>
> **SAME OR ANOTHER CHILD:** *We hear a lot of sounds when we go bowling: roll, bam, cheer, and crash.*

Then review the poem with the children.

Example:

> **TEACHER:** *There are many ways we could write a poem about bowling. Here's one of them:*
>
> > *I like to go bowling on Saturday.*
> > *My mom takes me to the lanes.*
> > *We hear a lot of sounds when we go bowling:*
> > *roll, bam, and crash.*

Practice

Provide the children with more practice composing poems with sound words.

■ Select an activity listed on the board.

■ Have the children compose sentences about it.

■ Discuss sound words and how they can write these in their poems.

Writing Poetry

Tell the children to write or say poetry about things, places, and activities that make many sounds. Review some of the topics. Tell them to use at least one sound word in their poems. It may be from the board, or they might think of a new one.

Making Art

The children then create art to imitate the sounds described in their poems. Give them a variety of objects that make sounds when they touch. Clothespins hung close together could sound like rain. Washers on a string might click and clang like a train chugging down the track.

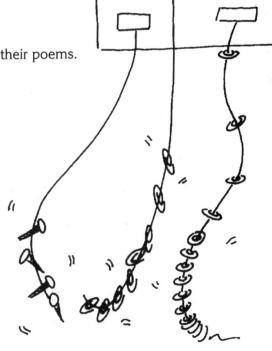

TORNADO

A tornado is like a tube,

making a howling noise,

whoosh!

Johannas Heller, age 6

A train goes, choo choo.
The wind says, whiss,
and the rain
sounds like beans falling.

Patricia Wreford-Brown, age 7

HONK, HONK

When a car starts its engine,

it rumbles, rumbles,

rroooms, rroooms.

It sounds like honk, honk

when it's stuck in traffic.

Then it rolls

and makes strange noises

like squealing mice,

squeak, squeak,

tumble, tumble.

Montana Tippett, age 8

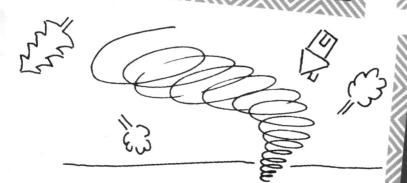

NIGHT

The tree is rustling in the night.

The night is black

like panthers that growl.

Paul Bruene, age 5

RAIN

Rain sounds like slippers
slapping on the floor.
Rain on top of a car
sounds like a ball bouncing.
Rain is quiet
like butterflies in the spring.

Sophie Baird-Daniel, age 5

From *Word Weavings: Writing Poetry with Young Children* published by Good Year Books. Copyright © 1997 Shelley Tucker.

Clanging Machines

Description

Some words sound like the sounds and actions they name. Listen to the words *brittle* break between the *ts*, *whirl* spin around on a breath, and *yo-yo* slide back and forth on its string of two words.

In this exercise, the children describe real or imagined machines and their sounds. Then they make machine masks to illustrate their poems.

Presentation

Ask the children to name actual and imaginary machines and list them on the board.

Examples:

car	*refrigerator*
airplane	*washing machine*
toaster	*clock*
computer	*dog walker*
bus	*homework machine*

Then have the children name some sounds machines make. List their responses on the board. They do not need to be grouped by category.

Examples:

roar	*tick tock*
roll	*hum*
twirl	*buzz*
pop	*ring*
click	*clang*
beep	

Choose a machine and have the children suggest the first line for a poem about it. Then ask some of the following questions to show them how to extend their ideas:

> *What does it do? How big is it? What color is it?*
> *What other machine does it look like?*
> *Who will tell us something more about this machine?*
> *What else does it do?*

Art Materials

- Tagboard, 6 by 8 inches (15.24 by 20.32 cm), 1 piece per child

- Pencils, crayons, or markers

- Hole punch

- Scissors

- String

- Things to create the appearance of machines, such as paper clips, bottle lids, buttons, aluminum foil

From *Word Weavings: Writing Poetry with Young Children* published by Good Year Books. Copyright © 1997 Shelley Tucker.

Example:	**CHILD:** *My machine gives my dog a bath.* **TEACHER:** *Who will give us another sentence about a machine that gives a dog a bath?* **SAME OR ANOTHER CHILD:** *It also dries the dog.* **TEACHER:** *What else does it do?* **SAME OR ANOTHER CHILD:** *It brushes the dog's teeth.*

Ask the children to describe the sounds of the machines, if they haven't yet.

Example:	**TEACHER:** *Who will suggest a sentence about the sounds that this machine makes?* **SAME OR ANOTHER CHILD:** *My machine swishes and swirls.*

Then review the whole poem.

Example:	*My machine gives my dog a bath.* *It also dries the dog* *and brushes the dog's teeth.* *My machine swishes and swirls.*

Practice

Provide the children with more practice by doing this exercise:

- Have the children suggest a first line about a machine.

- Ask them questions about it and have them answer in complete sentences.

- If the children haven't included sounds, ask them what sounds the machine makes. Then have them write these sounds in a separate sentence.

- Review the entire poem.

Writing Poetry

Tell the children to write poems about real or made-up machines. They describe how the machines look and what they do. Have them include at least one sound word. The children may use the sound words on the board or invent their own.

Making Art

Give each child a piece of tagboard. Holding the papers horizontally, measure and cut a place for their eyes. Have the children draw their machines on the paper, putting windows, wheels, or doors around the eye holes. After they cut out their machines, ask them to punch holes in the sides and thread the holes with string. Wearing their masks, the children can look out from the inside of their machines.

My machine helps hurt bunnies hop

and makes loud crackling sounds.

My machine washes clothes in a minute

and cleans the house in two minutes.

My machine makes gardens grow.

Allison Obourn, age 8

My machine washes the dishes.

It uses a lot of soap

and throws them into the air to dry.

Sometimes, my machine has problems.

Oh no!

Crash, splat, crack!

Ray Perez, age 8

SQUIRT

You put a rock in my machine

and it makes you a soda.

If you get greedy, it squirts you.

Briana du Nann, age 7

THE PLANE

The plane flies in the sky

and sounds like the ocean roaring.

When the plane lands

it is soft, ssh, ssh, ssh.

Then it rests, zzzzzzzz,

and is ready to go again.

Thomas Delarose, age 7

FINAL FOUR BASKETBALL

I have a Final Four machine.

It gives me pins and symbols,

hoops and basketballs,

and it sounds like

swish, swish, swish.

Raymond Leighton, age 6

From *Word Weavings: Writing Poetry with Young Children* published by Good Year Books. Copyright © 1997 Shelley Tucker.

References

Poetry

Adoff, Arnold. *In for Winter, Out for Spring.* San Diego: Harcourt Brace Jovanovich, 1991.

Fleischman, Paul. *Joyful Noise: Poems for Two Voices.* New York: Harper Trophy, 1988.

Kennedy, X. J., and Kennedy, Dorothy, eds. *Talking Like the Rain.* New York: Little Brown and Company, 1992.

Koch, Kenneth, and Farrell, Kate, eds. *Talking to the Sun.* New York: The Metropolitan Museum of Art, 1985.

Livingston, Myra Cohn. *Flights of Fancy and Other Poems.* New York: Simon and Schuster, 1994.

Livingston, Myra Cohn, and Fisher, Leonard Everett. *Festivals.* New York: Holiday House, 1996.

Nye, Naomi Shihab. *The Tree Is Older Than You Are.* New York: Simon and Schuster, 1995.

Schwartz, Alvin. *A Twister of Twists, A Tangler of Tongues.* Philadelphia: J. B. Lippincott Company, 1972.

Stafford, William. *Stories That Could Be True.* New York: Harper and Row, 1977.

Sullivan, Charles, ed. *Imaginary Gardens.* New York: Times Mirror, 1989.

Worth, Natalie. *all the small poems.* New York: Farrar, Straus and Giroux, 1987.

Art

Amery, Heather. *Fun with Paper.* New York: Reed International Books Ltd., 1994.

Barry, Jan. *Draw, Design, and Paint.* Parsippany, NJ: Good Apple, 1990.

Brackett, Karen, and Manley, Rosie. *Beautiful Junk: Creative Classroom Uses for Recyclable Materials.* Carthage, IL: Fearon Teacher Aids, 1990.

Milord, Susan. *Adventures in Art.* Charlotte, VT: Williamson Publishing, 1990.

Schonzeit, Marcia, ed. *Month by Month Arts and Crafts.* New York: Scholastic Professional Books, 1991.

Terzian, Alexandra M. *Kids' Multicultural Art Book.* Charlotte, VT: Williamson Publishing, 1993.

Bookmaking

Chapman, Gillian, and Robson, Pam. *Making Books.* Brookfield, CT: The Millbrook Press, 1991.

Evans, Joy, and Moore, Jo Ellen. *How to Make Books with Children.* Volumes 1 and 2. Monterey, CA: Evan-Moor Corporation, 1991.

Irvine, Joan. *How to Make Pop-ups.* New York: The Beach Tree Paperback Book, 1987.

Walsh, Natalie. *Making Books Across the Curriculum.* New York: Scholastic Professional Books, 1994.

From *Word Weavings: Writing Poetry with Young Children* published by Good Year Books. Copyright © 1997 Shelley Tucker.